Struck by Reality

A Journey of Awakening

Karen Maharaj

BALBOA.PRESS

A DIVISION OF HAY HOUSE

Balboa Press books may be ordered through booksellers or by contacting:

Balboa Press
A Division of Hay House
1663 Liberty Drive
Bloomington, IN 47403
www.balboapress.com
1 (877) 407-4847

Because of the dynamic nature of the Internet, any web addresses or
links contained in this book may have changed since publication and
may no longer be valid. The views expressed in this work are solely those
of the author and do not necessarily reflect the views of the publisher,
and the publisher hereby disclaims any responsibility for them.

The author of this book does not dispense medical advice or prescribe the use
of any technique as a form of treatment for physical, emotional, or medical
problems without the advice of a physician, either directly or indirectly. The
intent of the author is only to offer information of a general nature to help
you in your quest for emotional and spiritual well-being. In the event you use
any of the information in this book for yourself, which is your constitutional
right, the author and the publisher assume no responsibility for your actions.

Any people depicted in stock imagery provided by Getty Images are
models, and such images are being used for illustrative purposes only.
Certain stock imagery © Getty Images.

Print information available on the last page.

ISBN: 978-1-9822-4704-1 (sc)
ISBN: 978-1-9822-4705-8 (e)

Balboa Press rev. date: 06/01/2020

To James William Barton, who is forever in my heart.

Contents

Acknowledgments

To everyone I have encountered in my life, I have grown and seen life more clearly through these eyes and you are all my reflections as I am yours. Thank you for being a part of my journey.

To the whole universe and life, all of my angels, arch angels, saints and spirit guides, ancestors and especially my Dad Haniff, James and Audrey...Thank you

To everyone I've worked with on this project at Balboa Press, thank you. Thank you for communicating with me often, for the work that was done on my manuscript and for this process being straight forward and attainable. To my Editor Holly, for all the time and effort you invested in Struck by Reality. Thank you. You have inspired me to complete another story book I worked on a few years ago. To the design team, thank you for the beautiful, flawless cover designed for Struck by Reality.

Danny, first for being my friend as we worked through traumatic, lifechanging events and showing me what love really is, thank you. And thank you for the way you are with me, always caring about what I think feel and what goes on in my heart. Thank you for sharing our time with JR and having so many quality moments together. I love you.

Marie, thank you for always being my sister and my friend and holding me close to your heart. For the way we are with each other, for sharing your heart with me and being so gentle when I share. For dropping everything when you were ill on June 24, 2018, driving two hours to pick me up at the hospital after the accident. For calling me everyday after the accident and insisting that I receive medical attention when I refused to do so. Thank you for encouraging me to complete my book and always believing in me. Thank you for the amazing work you have done to bring me up to speed with Social Media and for managing my Website. Thank you for sharing the experience of being in Calvin's life. I love you.

Stu, thank you for your friendship and for being there when I needed financial advice and helping me crunch the numbers. Thank you for urging me to have hope and reminding me that I don't know what the future holds.

Maureen, for embracing me so many times while having panic attacks and reminding me that I am strong and not a victim, thank you. Thank you for being by my side through all the Grady projects and legal paperwork. I am grateful for our friendship. I love you

Angie T, for always making my hair beautiful. For all the fun times we have spent together celebrating birthdays and all the good times to come. Thank you, I love you.

Erica H, thank you for giving me guidance on all the legal paperwork we needed to complete and for being a friend. Thank you for the many times we get together and the fun that we have.

Marianne, thank you for the strong bond and friendship we have nurtured since college. I love you

Louise T, thank you for the many heartfelt conversations and the transparency we have about so many topics we have discussed. Thank you for supporting me with this book and being there for me when Pepper passed away.

Dr. Flo Barber, thank you for being a mentor and an inspiration to follow my heart and become a published author. Thank you for your healing work with cranio-somatic therapy, which has helped me to function when I have migraines and physical pain.

Jamie, at Dr. Barber's office for your bright spirit and positive outlook. Thank you! For always having a hopeful disposition when I come into the office for CranioSomatic therapy and always following up on me. And for completing and submitting all the paperwork. Thank you.

Michael Brady, thank you for past-life regression / healing work and a deeper spiritual perspective about my connection with James. Thank you for holding my hand as I navigated the spiritual plane to find answers about my karmic connection with James.

Michelle Trippi and the other unnamed stranger, thank you for performing CPR on James on the beach, regardless of inclement weather.

Thank you to Sarasota County Emergency Services

Lifeguard Captain Roy Routh for your efforts to save James's life.

Sarasota County Fire medics, thank you for CPR and your attempts to save James's life.

Thank you to all the first responders for trying to save James's life.

Thank you to the chaplain and detectives at Sarasota Memorial for helping me to get through those difficult moments at the hospital.

Tony Morrero, *Tampa Bay Times* writer, thank you for reaching out to me and patiently allowing me to share our story. Thank you for writing the story exactly as I told it. Thank you for following up and being so kind in those initial days after the accident.

Karen Mertes, for friendship and for helping me to understand what Traumatic Brain Injury is and how to help myself heal. Thank you and Fulfill Your Destiny for the grant toward publishing this book.

Dr. Toms, Thank you for creating a space for me to be safe and comfortable to share openly with you. Thank you for your guidance and mostly for being patient.

Dr. Reddy, thank you for following my health and following up with me constantly. Thank you for the countless letters and referrals your office provided regarding my health care.

Felicia at Dr. Reddy's office. Thank you for always being kind and understanding and for submitting countless requests for paperwork.

Dr. Ahmed, thank you for being patient and understanding when it was often so difficult for me to understand what was going on inside of and around me. I appreciate all you have done to help me function on a day to day basis.

Tracy and Jamie at Dr. Ahmed's office, thank you for always helping when I call with questions for the assistance with paperwork.

Dr. Giuisti, thank you for caring and listening and helping me through all of life's changes.

Dr. Pages, thank you for TMS therapy and for your and your staff's compassionate care throughout my healing.

Brianna, Sydney, Amy at Dr. Pages office, I appreciate your kindness and I am grateful for TMS.

Dr. Donnell, thank you for helping me understand what I was experiencing. Thank you for caring and looking underneath to determine what was going on with my health.

Lynn, Thank you for referring me to Dr. Ann Witt for always checking on me and being supportive

Dr. Ann Witt, for ART therapy which was so powerful when Pepper passed away. Thank you.

TGH, for all the support you have given me throughout my employment.

Brenda, thank you for being my dear friend and for sharing and allowing me to share in my most vulnerable moments. Thank you for all your advice.

Shawn W, thank you for standing by my side through two divorces and always loving me. Thank you for the beautiful friendship we have had over the years. I love you

Matt W, thank you for being a brother to me and embracing me as family.

Portia, for your loving friendship and holding each others hearts as if it was our own. Thank you for all the wonderful times we've spent together. Thanks for always being a bright light in my life and helping me to gain perspective when I am hurting. I love you

Aunt Prema, thank you for always caring and calling to check on me and for checking on my health. Thank you for being gentle when life is too much to handle and for always being a mom to me. I love you

Thank you, Uncle Haro, for embracing me, bringing me closer to family and for reminding me that I am not pumpkin vine ☺family. I love you

Aunt Zira, thank you for giving me feedback on my manuscript.

Xai, thank you for being my harshest critic. I am clear about my purpose and more determined to honor James' life

Janet K and Gary K, thank you for embracing me and giving Danny and I your blessings.

Merlin G, for being my lifelong friend and always tracking me down and caring. Thank you for bringing me to Maajii when I was at rock bottom in my life. Thank you for always being there for me in my frustrating moments. Thank you for the many joyful memories we have shared and for all the ways we have fulfilled our childhood promise to always be close and supportive of each other. Thank you for embracing me no matter how bad things have gotten and for always reminding me that the spiritual path will set me free.

Maaji, thank you for reading my Patra and guiding me through dark moments. For all of the Poojas and prayers you've said for me, thank you.

Jessica K, thank you for encouraging me to be the full expression of myself and for introducing me to Michael Brady. You will publish your book also!

Yasmirys, Thank you for Reiki, massage, yoga and deeper spiritual understanding. Thank you for teaching me to be gentler with myself.

Wilson, for pet-sitting our babies while we are gone

Christine, for friendship and for pet-sitting the pets over the years. Thank you.

Cynthia, thank you for being a friend and sister and always checking on me while I was out on medical leave. Thank you for your prayers. Thank you for always reminding me to be hopeful.

Miranda and Crystal, y'all made it fun at TGH.

Angelo, thank you for all the lessons we shared.

Reshma, for always being a loving cousin. Thank you!

Evemarie and Ron S, for all the good times we have shared, thank you. Thank you for your kindness throughout the last couple years. Thank you for the lovely vacation we had in Punta Cana.

Cousins Donald, Michelle, and Annie, thank you for your kindness while I was in Trinidad visiting after the accident

Fred Eppsteiner, for guidance and clarity on mindfulness, being in awareness and so many truths about reality. Thank you for silent retreats and the wisdom you've imparted on me.

Thank you to Rebecca Campbell for connecting me with Hayhouse UK. I am so grateful for your work and your powerful presence.

To all my sisters from the Rise Sister Rise Workshop, thank you for lovingly embracing me when I showed up at Omega to the workshop broken and distraught.

All members of the Florida Community of Mindfulness, thank you for embracing me in the mindfulness community

To all my friends and family, for loving me even though I have changed in so many ways after June 24, 2018. Thank you

Foreword

When Karen Maharaj first contacted me in my capacity as a Past Life Therapist, I was unaware of her recent experience of being struck by lightning. I had missed it going by in the local news. When I learned that her companion James had died in that same experience, I knew it was important for me to work with her in healing from such a trauma. In my work over the past 39 years, I have been especially concerned with helping my clients understand and heal wounds in their karmic relationships with important people in their lives. James was certainly one such person for Karen. Traumas like this can wound and incapacitate a person for the rest of their life. Or transform them in some ways and mark the positive unfolding of the rest of their life. For Karen, this certainly turned out to be the latter. I was genuinely surprised during our early sessions to discover that James had "hung around" after his death.

The transcripts of these sessions provide the reader the rare opportunity to experience what it was really like to be there. The emotional catharsis and healing can be felt again as the reader goes along for the ride with Karen!

The book is a way to accompany Karen in her daily life, while she is searching for and determining the meaning of her life. She happens to have some extraordinary experiences happen along the way that transforms everything for her. This is a powerful personal account of her journey that will touch you deeply. Don't be surprised if you find yourself reading the book more than once!

Michael Brady B.S. M.A.

Discovering Your Soul Mission By Linda and Michael Brady

Introduction

This book does not contain instructions on how to achieve your spiritual goals. Nor does it provide "how-to" guidelines for your personal growth. This book was born in my heart on December 31, 2017, while I was driving to a New Year's Eve ceremony at my local Community of Mindfulness center. My heart opened up as I became clear that I was beginning my personal journey of awakening to the reality of life as it was in front of me. The only other details I knew at that time was that I needed to write about my spiritual awakening over the next year and the writing must be done in the present moment to reflect on life as it occurred.

The significance of writing about life as it unfolded would be my personal experiment to determine which truth was sustainable for me—the one in my mind that had been fueled by traditions, belief systems, norms, and societal expectations or the reality in front of me. I knew that this would require a lot of trust. It would require a shift in my paradigm for life. I would have to really trust that life was for me.

At this point in my life, I felt like I had no other choice. I'd been beaten down, and the old model just hadn't worked for me. I was willing to try something different. Even if it didn't work, I knew that I could exercise my option to free myself of all the "shoulds" that I had so dearly attached myself to up until this point in my life.

I had chosen to be present and mindful, with life in front of me, and to let go of any desires and expectations in my life. I had decided to just *be*. Practicing this over the next year would help me to decide which truth worked best for me. The key to the process was that I would be writing about the journey as it occurred and, therefore, living in the moment. The name of this book—*Struck by Reality*—unfolded as part of the process of being with life as it unfolded.

I started this journey, and I am sharing my experience with you to inspire you to look for and to take the path less traveled. I am sharing this because I know that the next stage in my growth involves being an example of living life authentically. I am committing to this process because I believe that we all have a unique contribution and gift to share within our lifetime. Self-discovery is the only path on which we can discover our gifts, if we are willing to go there. I hope this will help you to find and trust the voice that speaks within your heart.

I believe that the spiritual pioneers leading us to the next level of spiritual growth on planet earth will gently guide us back on a journey within ourselves, with the understanding that all that we need to know and learn first comes from within. I believe that the model we will follow will be experiential in nature—you can see what I did and try it, maybe it will help you on your path. Do as I do, not do as I say.

Awake

I woke up to a state of constant joy.
And I know that this will never
leave me.
Nor will it be tarnished
by any outside judgment of me.
I got my wish to be fully present and awake.
Sometimes, we must hit
rock bottom.
And when we
think we're at the lowest point,
get knocked down even harder, in order to see
and understand deeply that our true
nature is when we have chosen to exist
in a state of joy in the present moment.
I now know with 100 percent certainty that I
can let go of any thoughts that hold me prisoner to life.

—Karen Maharaj, Self-Reflection, December 20, 2018

Chapter 1

Facing Reality

. . . .

Make me strong in spirit,
courageous in action ... let me act in wisdom,
conquer my fear and doubt, discover my own hidden gifts,
meet others with compassion, be a source of healing energies, and
face each day with hope and joy.

—Abby Willowroot

January 2, 2018

The last year of my marriage, my husband and I were adopting a baby. After working through the adoption paperwork and the process for the entire previous year, our adoption profile was posted at the beginning of May 2017. Shortly after in June, we were matched. It was surprisingly perfect, and I was overjoyed. I had waited for this moment the entire five years of our marriage. My dream of having my own little family was materializing, and it seemed like we were meant to adopt because we were matched in such a short period of time. This was after having much difficulty trying to have a baby naturally.

Our second year of marriage to each other started with an ectopic pregnancy in 2012. Then there was a miscarriage in 2013. In April and October 2015, we had two failed rounds of in vitro fertilization (IVF). I was emotionally, mentally, and physically exhausted. We waited six months after our second failed IVF session before deciding to move forward with the adoption process. I was finally seeing the light at the end of tunnel. The baby was due on September 4, 2017. But based on the birth mom's history, she was expected to deliver around week thirty-six. *Wow!* Our baby was going to be here by mid-August.

I flew to Trinidad on my birthday, July 21, 2017. My dad had his third stroke that year and was paralyzed on the right side of his body. It was difficult to see him like that; it affected me deeply. I returned home from Trinidad July 24 upset and emotional about the condition of my dad. It seemed like he was unstable. And in my heart, I was dreading the idea that he would not be here much longer. I missed my connecting flight in Fort Lauderdale, and there wasn't another flight until the next day. That night, I sat in the hotel room and processed everything inside of me with much difficulty, accepting the condition I'd seen my dad in.

There was a bittersweet aspect of what was going on inside of me because I was terrified of losing my dad and excited to get home. In the meantime, the adoption agency contacted my husband and shared that they knew the sex of the baby. He insisted that we hear the news together and scheduled a call for late evening July 25, 2017. That evening as I arrived home, we learned that the baby was a girl. I was overjoyed. In the coming days we decided to name her Sophia.

On the evening of July 28, 2017, it felt like I had been shaken awake from a dream I'd been having for years—at least seven years. Weeks before the baby was due, my husband expressed how he really felt about me. It was such a rude awakening. I realized that what I'd thought was a happy marriage was only a fantasy, which I was experiencing in my own mind. *But this can't be happening to me*, I thought. *I am the perfect wife, and we have a wonderful life together.*

That night I faced reality, and it was the hardest thing to accept. What I heard could not be unheard. As I sat in my room night after night, I realized this may have been my husband's way of telling me he didn't want to be a dad, and that he was terrified. Instead, his words sounded different. I felt like I was being belittled, demeaned, and betrayed. Suddenly I was defending myself as to why I would be a good mother.

I had two choices. Either I could go on pretending that everything was okay and bring baby Sophia into our unbalanced world, or I could wake up and realize this was not my path and walk away from this situation. The awakening was like a jolt of lightning through my body. So much came up for me in those silent moments night after night. I realized my own personal history was repeating itself. Did my dad drive off with me when I was two and a half years old and not return me to my mom because he thought she was not capable of being a good mom? I made peace in my heart with my mom because I finally understood the pain she'd withstood. All the causes to the conditions in my life came up, whether I was willing or ready to have an awareness of them.

It was clear to me that I needed to decide what was in the best interest of the baby. It was also obvious that what I'd thought regarding the reality of my marriage was not what was actually happening. I realized that baby Sophia needed to be in a home where both parents were ecstatic to have her, and who wanted to give her the best of everything in life to help her and guide her. I would have to make this decision alone. And the choice I made would determine the fate of this innocent unborn baby. This would impact her entire life.

It was an internal battle between everything I dreamed about creating in my life—having my own family—and the reality that the choice to bring baby Sophia home would not be one made in partnership. At least we were not partners in the sense that I had *thought* we were in this process. These were thoughts I believed, but my reality was not congruent with my thoughts.

I could be selfish and become a mom. My heart was heavy. I was reminded that I couldn't be responsible for contributing to a situation where both parties were not equally invested in the desired outcome—especially where another innocent life was concerned. Maybe my own personal history contributed to this understanding.

In the coming month, I spent my days working and my evenings processing my life situation. I cut off all communication with my friends and family. I allowed myself time to be silent to process everything. I knew I would make the right decisions with the knowledge, understanding, and awareness I had in those moments. I'd always believed our marriage was solid. There was love and togetherness. I needed to know that we had a solid foundation as a couple before starting a family. I'd believed that, even if we didn't have a child, we could spend the rest of our lives being happy and loving each other. During the entire process of adoption, when we'd often felt overwhelmed, I had assured my husband that I was willing to give up the whole idea of having a baby. I reassured him that I felt like a baby would be an *addition* to our already happy life. It was very important to me that the adoption process was a partnership between us and that we truly went into it wholeheartedly. I knew we could be happy together without a child because we were solid in our own foundation as a couple—or so I'd thought.

I had been caught up in my fantasy of a happy life. I'd never seen how my marriage really was. I had to face the truth about my situation.

On August 10, the adoption agency reached out to us. The baby's birth was going to be the next day or possibly over the weekend. That evening I returned the call and informed the agency that we were not going through with the adoption.

On November 16, 2017, we were divorced.

The Road Not Taken

Two roads diverged in a wood, and I—
I took the one less traveled by,
And that has made all the difference.

—Robert Frost

Chapter 2

Reflecting

. . . .

The aspirations and intentions of the present moment is more
powerful than everything that happened in the past.
—Fred Eppsteiner

January 4, 2018

On July 28, 2017, one of the questions my ex-husband asked me was why I meditated. He suggested that I try something different because what I was doing did not work. In that moment, I responded, "This is who I am!" I remember moving my right hand over my heart. I said, "This is inside of me, and I cannot change this. Nor will I ever want to change this."

I had finally claimed I was a spiritual being, and it seemed like, at that moment, the whole universe stepped in and took over. I was finally honest with myself about who I was. And it was freeing. I said it out loud. I was fully and completely accepting that I was a spiritual being having a human experience. Before that moment, there was a part of me that denied the spiritual practice I'd anchored my entire existence in. Despite fear, I trusted my connection to spirit as the driving force in my life. This was the foundation of my existence. I knew that everything I had in life, and all I had become, had come to me through spirit. At the core of my being, I lived from spirit. I went there to get my answers. And by "there," I mean within. I had always been guided by the universe and the force of life.

I was raised Catholic. I began meditating around age ten. I connected with source, and I knew that God was not a person in the sky. As I grew older, I realized that the essence of life was the thread that flows within everything.

Most of all, I know now that, if I really want to connect with the source of my being, then I must go within and be still long enough to experience the spaciousness and emptiness of my own being. That's when the answers come. This is how I got to this point in my life. I had to go it all alone, and I didn't always make the best decisions, but I always received guidance from within. I always had a spiritual practice.

I had known this most of my life. But I hadn't had the courage to tell my moms, who are Catholic and Pentecostal, that I am not a Christian. I hadn't had the courage to say to most people in my life that I am not anything, and I am everything. I accept truths from different paths as my own because I believe that, ultimately, we are all part of one greater consciousness, and we each shape how we express this greater consciousness through the filter of our life experience. Most importantly, I believe that the path I choose is a choice that only I can make. I believe that is truth for everyone else also. I don't need to convince anyone to believe, think, or act as I do. If my actions and words are aligned with truth, then I will be an example for others with whom I interact. By doing so, I am accepting and allowing life to be as it is, knowing that we are all unique, and that's what was meant to be.

One of the reasons for the ending of our first marriage was my spirituality. At the time, I was studying *A Course in Miracles*. I am quite intense about everything I do. I spent years walking around with that blue book. A course that is structured to be completed in one year, with lessons setup for each day of the year, took me about four years. This was because I practiced each lesson until I felt like I had gotten it. I never tried to share my beliefs in my relationship with my ex-husband. Nor did I ever get offended when he picked up Post-It notes with affirmations and hid them away when friends or family came over. I figured most people would think I was weird, and part of me felt weird for being so deeply attached to needing spiritual food daily. It was the one thing I knew to be my constant throughout my life. Even as a child, I craved understanding things at a deeper level. I aspired to understand the deeper meaning of life. I read and listened to books on audio from spiritual teachers such as Wayne Dyer, Louise Hay, and Deepak Chopra. There was a part of me that didn't accept me for who I was, and that part of me was willing to hide.

It was not until I was in Trinidad in July sitting with my dad and holding his hand for those three days that it finally hit me. Most of the time, I just sat by his side and waited for my dad to speak. When he did, I listened. I wanted to soak in every moment with him and take in everything he had to say. My dad lay in his bed and gazed off in the distance. At one point, he turned to me and told me he was seeing a vision. He then let me know he had been seeing visions since he was a little boy.

My dad had been a vegetarian his entire life. If you met him, the first thing he would say to you is, "I have been a vegetarian my entire life. I have never eaten an egg since birth. I obey the commandment of thou shalt not kill. That is my religion."

I have heard him say that over and over thousands of times over many years. I asked him what he was seeing. Dad asked me if my husband and I were adopting a baby. I affirmed that we were. He then asked me if it was going to be a boy or a girl. I said we did not know yet. My dad looked off in the distance again, and then he looked at me and asked me what sex I wanted the baby to be. For the first time without hesitation I just blurted out, "A girl." We always said we wanted a healthy baby, and the sex didn't matter. But in that moment, something inside of me decided that I wanted a little girl. My dad looked away again, and then he looked at me and stated, "You are going to get what you want." I got back to Florida and we learned that the baby was a girl.

When my dad shared with me that he had been having visions since he was a little boy, I understood a little bit more about myself. And finally, the part of me that was denying and hiding the fact that everything I had done up to this point in my life had been sourced by spirit finally decided to accept me for me. My dad explained that his grandfather was a very spiritual man and he'd learned everything from him. I realized that all my ancestors' yearning for an understanding of the undercurrents of life was also in me. It became clearer that I had been hungry for and grounded in my spiritual path because this was *who I am*. This was part of my identity. It was in every cell of my body.

I realize now that it was not possible to be seen for who I am before that moment by anyone else because I had to first see myself and claim my own divinity for others to see me. Once I accepted myself and my yearning for deeper spiritual understanding, I gave up control of my life to the universe. I was no longer in the driver's seat. I was no longer goal setting, wishing, wanting, and grasping. I didn't know what the next step was, and I had no need to know. I got it! Life had been knocking on my door. Every experience was an opportunity to wake up in my own life. And I didn't heed the call initially.

Now, I have no agendas and no need to plan or have a sense of direction. I am just going to get up and face each new day with curiosity and see what happens. I've had this amazing feeling of freedom and spaciousness within me lately. I feel lighter because I have released the burden of keeping up with the "should bes" of life. I am at peace. Looking back now, it was like I woke up from a dream and realized that what I thought was best for me was all an illusion. I was reaching, wanting, and grasping so desperately for this family life, for this baby that I could not conceive. When it finally came together, it all fell apart so quickly. It was not the path for me.

I met my friend Marie for dinner in early September. It was right around her birthday. I explained to her what had happened and how difficult the decision not to adopt was for me. Marie and I had been on a similar spiritual path. She and I sat at my kitchen table week after week for a year while I became certified as an Emotional Freedom Technique (EFT) practitioner, and we tapped away all our issues. We'd always read similar books. Since she devoured books, it was always Marie who updated me on the spiritual books I had to read next.

As more came out over the coming months, Marie, being a sister to me, held me gently and searched for everything that could help me get through this period of my life. Marie spends time listening to audio books on Audible early in the morning before her son wakes up. Here are some texts she sent me with suggestions for books I needed to read to help me through my current life changes:

> September 23, 5:59 a.m.
> *Seven Cups of Consciousness* by Aleya Dao. I think you would like that book.

> October 14, 8:36 a.m.
> Hi, Sis. I'm reading two books I can't put down (actually listening on Audible). *The 5 Second Rule*— not spiritual but sooo good application of everyday courage, book with great stories. I just started *Moonology*. It's cool. Just wanted to share. Love you.

> October 15, 10:30 p.m.
> After you shared with me what your dad said about his book of secrets, I did some research and came across *The Book of Secrets* by Deepak Chopra. OMG this book is amazing. Need to talk to you about it. He talks about getting a reading (reluctantly) from an Indian guy. Lots of very deep quantum physics stuff. I feel like I'm going to listen to this book ten times. There's so much powerful stuff in it. Forget about my two other recommendations. Grab this one if you feel guided to do so.

November 16, 9:08 p.m.
Hay House is in Tampa in April!

And here's a reply from me. On November 24 at 12:11 p.m., I wrote:

Going to listen to *Spirit Junkie* while I work.

Marie's recommendations kept coming:

November 24, 12:11 p.m.
I am so glad you like the book! I thought you would. I read *The Universe Has Your Back*, and I did not like it. Strange, right? I guess I wasn't ready to hear it when I read it. But I love *Spirit Junkie*.

Here are some recommendations:

Instant Healing by a Hawaiian guy, Serge Kahili.

Loving What Is by Byron Katie.

Disappearance of the Universe, another great one. This is a channeled reading, very interesting, completely different from all the other books.

Gabriel Bernstein is coming up with a new book in a few weeks called *Judgment Detox*. I bet it's going to be awesome.

November 27, 4:49 a.m.
Been up since 3. Another absolute read from the first minute—*Light is the New Black* by Rebecca Campbell. Forget about the other books. You must get this book. Return a book if you must.

Omg, this is talking to you and me. I'm crying right now. You have to hear this.

Omg, she's talking now about silent retreats and Saint Francis.

When you are done with your book, I want to refer you to a publisher.

The biggest candle casts the biggest shadow.

This book is better than the last two combined.

December 13, 6:18 a.m.

You are a writer. We are going to be celebrating your book. I know it in my soul.

December 14, 4:50 p.m.

Rise Sister Rise is even more for you, I think. She talks about *Healing Your Life* by Louise Hay and also Shakti awakening. This book is fascinating, I think you will relate."

December 15, 5:30 p.m.

I Measure My Success By How Much Fun I'm having.

I woke up to life!

When I woke up, all I heard within me was *be here now*. Be present in this moment. Slowly learn to get out of your mind and be mindful and aware of what is going on in and around you. Be patient. Be patient through this process because you are undoing a lifetime of living in your head where what you think is reality is not reality. What you are seeing in front of you is real, so be with it fully. Experience it through all your senses. This is the only reality. Pay attention. There is no other reality.

I attended my second silent retreat with the local Community of Mindfulness on October 26–30, 2017. It was at the Franciscan Center on the Hillsborough River. I arrived on Thursday around

4:00 p.m., and as I settled in, I sat on my bed and wrote down my intentions.

The next day, at 6:45 a.m., I met with the center leader in a small group and expressed that I had intentions of letting go of so much by the end of this retreat. Fred asked me what was stopping me from letting go of this right now and enjoying the rest of the retreat. I looked at him with amazement and, in that moment, gave myself permission to let it all go. There was a sense of relief, and it felt like a weight had been lifted off my shoulders.

It was just choosing to let go in that moment that freed me. The truth is, I am empowered to make that choice from moment to moment to be free of the past. The past is no longer reality. It is gone. What is real is only in the present moment.

As the retreat progressed, I heard Fred say over and over that we needed to understand "the nature of the mind." The more aware we are of the thoughts we have and the natural inclination to be stuck in the past the more empowered we are to make the choice that frees us. That choice is the choice to breathe in the present moment and to be fully aware, with all our senses, what is going on right now.

I had been ready to give myself four days of wallowing time to dwell on the recent events of my life—to really feel sorry for myself and suffer. And when I just let it go in that moment, I felt so free. I realized that, whether I am here now present in this moment or stuck in the past is a moment by moment choice. I don't have to choose suffering. I understand now that the nature of my mind is to dwell in the past, to hold on to what has already happened. And the stronger the emotions are around the experiences of my life, the more I tend to want to dwell on them. I am making a conscious effort to *choose* first—the choices that allow me to retrain the nature of my mind. I am choosing to be still and to be okay with what is going on in this moment, without looking to the past or reaching for something in the future.

This is how I wake up to the fullness of my life now. On December 31 at the Beginning Anew ceremony, Fred reminded us,

"The aspirations and intentions of the present moment are more powerful than everything that happened in the past."

At this point in my life, all my actions, conscious or unconscious, have resulted in my current life conditions. The causes have created conditions. The scales are balanced. I can move forward in life, creating each day fresh and new. I am choosing to give out only what I will want to have returned, because I know now that my life is a mirror. What I see in my outer world is a mirror of me, my inner world. Most importantly, I have the awareness that I must live awake fully in each moment, being aware of what is going on in my mind because my thoughts contribute to the causes and conditions I experience in my reality. By choosing to be here in the moment and experience what is in front of me without being consumed by the flooding of thoughts moving through my mind, I can set myself free of the causes and conditions and slowly become more familiar with the space within me. I have been practicing this. It truly feels like mission impossible and requires an incredible amount of patience. However, I am already feeling the rewards of being just a little awake in life, and I am seeing conditions reflecting at me that create a life of joy and peace. I feel at ease in life. I feel so loved by my friends and family. I feel supported. I relate to everything around me because I am first aware and connected with the spaciousness within me.

Life is simple and easy, and I don't have a clue what is going to happen next. I have decided to make the coming year my journey of becoming awake in my own existence, and I am going to write about this process. I've decided to do what makes me happy and what brings me joy in each moment. I will be present with the struggles that come up so that I can accept and allow them to pass through me. I paint in my free time, and when I paint, I become consumed with what I am painting. I look at every line and curve. I've learned to see the different colors and textures in the objects I paint. I create contrast and can see the shadows. I write because I am a very introspective person, and by writing, I can process what I am experiencing in a way that brings value to my life. I lay on the couch with my two birds, Pepper and Petey, every day. We interact. I pet and love them. And in return, they love me in a way that fills me up. I spend time with my friends, laughing, talking, going out to dinner, and hiking. I notice so many special moments shared.

This is what I have. This day. This hour. This minute. This moment. All these aware moments create more aware moments in my life. And by making the effort to slowly be here more and more in each moment, I have chosen to wake up to life.

Poem from *Rise Sister Rise*

It's your humanness that inspires me:
The day you let your old self die, in order for who you were
becoming to be born.
It's your humanness that inspires me:
How no matter how many times you doubted it,
You never stopped answering the call.

—Rebecca Campbell

Chapter 3

Surrendering

. . . .

Wherever life's path leads you,
May every step along the way
Be filled with peace and courage.

—unknown

January 8, 2018

My pet green-cheeked conure, Pepper, passed away on the night of January 6, 2018. Pepper had been in my life for the last nineteen years. This was a long- term committed relationship. Pepper was very loving, and she was so loyal to me.

Pepper hadn't been flexible enough to preen herself in at least the last year or two. Birds have a preening gland at the back of their bodies by their tails that produces oils. These oils are essential for keeping their feathers healthy. Birds reach back, rub their heads in the oils and then rub their heads over all areas of their bodies, distributing the oils onto their feathers. Lately Pepper's flexibility had been so diminished that I'd been giving her baths every other day to wash off the buildup in her preening gland, keeping her clean since she had not been able to preen herself. Pepper and I had a daily routine. This involved giving her the meloxicam prescribed by her vet an hour before her bath, and then washing off the area around her uropygial gland of any scabs or debris. Next, I would remove the scabs from the oils that were formed around the preening gland. This was very uncomfortable for her, and it broke my heart to see her suffer like this. After bathing Pepper, I usually lowered the setting on the blow dryer to dry her feathers and keep her warm. Even though I used warm water, she was usually shivering after her bath.

She snuggled up on my chest slightly under my chin and closed her eyes while making gentle cooing sounds. She really enjoyed the heat from the blow dryer. This was the best part of the routine for both of us. I started blow drying her feathers when I noticed how much she quivered from being cold from her daily baths.

On Saturday night, my good friends Shawn and Matt were over, and we all played with Pepper. Pepper was very loving toward Shawn and Matt. I watched her snuggle in Matt's hand and give Shawn kisses. She gave me kisses before going to bed, and I covered her cage and watched her for a while. The three of us played a game called The Transformation Game. As we played the game, we were astonished by the accuracy of the game in parallel to our lives. I had a lot of pain cards. I faced so much of my stuff, and we were lovingly and compassionately transformed in front of each other. I couldn't believe this game was really mirroring our lives. Matt went home, and Shawn spent the night.

I woke up Sunday morning, while Shawn was still sleeping and proceeded to the back room to bring the birds out. It was around 7:00 a.m. I reached down for Pepper at the bottom of her nighttime cage and noticed she was not responding. I picked her up. Her body was warm, and I rushed into the room and woke Shawn up, letting her know that Pepper was not responding. We rushed to the vet.

When we arrived, the staff at the vet's office looked at Pepper and took her back. Shortly after, they came out and informed me that Pepper was gone. They asked if I wanted to take her home. I nodded yes. I asked Shawn to contact my ex-husband and ask him to come over. I sobbed. This was not happening. I could lose everything in life but not Pepper. Noooooo!

When the vet brought her out in that little box, I felt the whole universe cave in on me. We got home, and my ex showed up. He was kind. He mentioned that I had given her the best life and that I had been the best mom to her. He asked me to pick out a spot in the backyard where I would want to bury her. He dug a hole. In the meantime, Matt arrived and instinctively brought a shoebox with him. It was good thinking, since the box Pepper was in seemed so small. They transferred her to the larger box. I placed her in her "snuggle buddies" that she'd snuggled up next to day after day.

Shawn asked me to let them know when I was ready.

I said, "I will never be ready."

It was around noon when we buried her. I drew the blinds, lay on the couch, and felt a heaviness in my being. It felt like a mountain of bricks were being laid on my chest.

***

You will seek the elixir in friends, lovers, enemies, books, religions, foreign countries, heroes' songs, rituals, and jobs, but no matter where you look the treasure will evade you. All will seem lost, and you will lose all hope that this magic potion even exists. This will be the darkest of nights, and the promise of certain death will lead you to the abyss of despair. But staring into the abyss you will see the dim light of your own illuminated soul. Your radiance will transform the abyss into the elusive elixir of life, and for the first time you will realize that all the while it was your own Light that you've been searching for.

—Mastin Kipp, *Claim Your Power*

***

Dear Universe,

I cannot handle any more pain in my life. I know you want me to be here now and feel everything, and I am. Please, please, please give me kind and gentle life lessons going forward. I can't take it anymore. I am asking you for a miracle.

Thank you,
Karen

Chapter 4

Acknowledging

. . . .

Pepper and Petey

Pepper on Ladder

January 12, 2018, 2:38 a.m.

My sweet angel Pepper,

I miss you my darling. These past days have been so hard because I am lost without you. I feel like my heart has been ripped out of my chest, and I am so empty inside. There is so much to thank you for. You were my constant for the last nineteen years. Thank you for being with me through all of life's changes.

Thank you for being so devoted and loyal to me. Thank you for coming back even when you accidentally flew out on three separate occasions. I know you came back because you wanted to be with me and love me, and I thank you for that. The first time you flew into a tree across the street from my mom's development, we climbed up a ladder, and you came right to us.

The second time, we'd just moved into Post Apartments. You sat on your cage all day while I worked. The apartment was dark, and when I opened the door, you flew toward the light in the hallway. I know that this was instinctual for you. You flew through the opening of the building, and I saw you fly off so fast around the buildings. It was dark. I stayed in the parking lot calling out to you screaming and crying, "Pepper, come back." I was like a crazy lady. I am realizing now that everyone in the entire apartment complex must have heard me. It didn't matter. After screaming your name at the top of my lungs for about twenty minutes, I decided to go onto my porch. I stood there crying, thinking I had lost you. Then I heard your little voice in the tree that was in front of the porch and you flew right onto my shoulder.

The third time, you flew out when we lived at Idlewild. The back door was open. I was sitting on the back steps. It seemed like your wings had been clipped recently. However, when you were about to hop onto my shoulder, you flew off not realizing your wings were fully grown. I remember we searched the neighborhood for you and called you. You were in a tree. You just dropped to the ground and allowed us to pick you up and bring you home. Thank you for your lifetime commitment to me, my sweet angel.

Thank you for the way you loved me. You were so sweet and gentle. You always gave me kisses. Thank you for the bedtime kisses every night for the last nineteen years when I put you to bed. Thank you for lying on my chest every evening for at least half an hour and for letting me pet you every day in the evening for the past three months since it's been just us here. Thank you for being patient with me when I bathe you. Thank you for taking your medicine that the doctor prescribed, even though I know you hated it. I know it helped with the pain. Thank you for still being spunky even after you lost your tail feathers in the last couple months when you were not able to fly.

Thank you for tolerating Petey and walking around on the floor and socializing with him lately. I know you had sixteen years of life with it being just us, before he came along. I thought you would be happy to have a friend. Thank you for seeing that Petey only wanted to love you and for letting him walk around with you on the floor. Thank you for being close to him in the last couple months when you could no longer fly.

He really misses you, and he is grieving also. He looks over in the morning at your cage because he always ate his breakfast when you were eating. He followed your lead on most things. He looks over at your bedtime cage when I roll his cage into the back room at night. He coos. He moves up and down his cage looking in your nighttime cage for you. I tried to take the cage away and put him in a different room, and he let me know he is not ready for that. I'm not ready for that either! I think your cages are going to stay where they are because we're more comfortable with things just the way they are, even though you are not here in the physical form. Somehow, I know you are here.

I want to dream of you every night. Thank you for letting us be here for each other in the past couple months since it's only been the three of us here. I know I could never give you enough for the love and stability that you have always given me. I thank you with my whole heart. There is something about your presence that always made me feel at ease in life and took my anxiety away. Thank you.

I am so grateful that I was out sick on January 3 and you snuggled up under my neck while we watched a movie in bed. It was so nice the way I stroked your feathers, and you made certain that your body was touching the skin of my face and neck, kissing my face and preening my hair. That was the longest stretch of alone time we have had together in a long while. I loved you so deeply, and you always loved me back. You loved me the way I needed to be loved. Thank you. You always reminded me that you were taking care of me by chirping to get my attention, and you always looked to see what Mommy was doing. I was at the center of your world. I also loved you more than I have loved most humans, and I'm not afraid to say that. Thank you for loving me so deeply and unconditionally.

We moved to nine different places together, some in a different state. I even left you in the care of Carol when I was at the Omega Institute for those seven months in 2006. You watched me get married and divorced twice. You watched me make all my decisions, good and bad, and you stood by my side. You slept behind a pillow in the bed with me for a long time. You saw me cry so many times, and when I cried, you hurt as much as I did. I remember you sitting on my pillow and preening my eyelashes so gently after you saw me crying. Thank you for your gentle loving reassurance over the years that things would be okay. No matter what happened in life, we had each other, and we knew we would get through anything because we were together. Thank you for believing in me and trusting me to love you and be the best mom to you.

In New York when we moved into the Martha Washington and mice were getting into the apartment, I was terrified for your well-being. Even after the problem was resolved, I had such a phobia of mice as a result of that experience that I left the sticky mice traps out. The thing that hurts me the most was that you somehow escaped from your cage while I was gone and got stuck in one of those. The amazing thing is that you wiggled your little body, losing some feathers getting free from the trap. You had a fighting spirit and amazing resilience. I knew you were traumatized by that experience and I loved you through it, and I am so sorry you had to go through that. I want you to know that that was when I decided to leave New York and move back to Florida.

You have always been dedicated to me, thank you so much. I want you to know that I was also always dedicated to your happiness and you were and will always be my number one. No one will have the space in my heart where you live. You are always in my heart, my love.

I remember the way we danced when we were alone, when you would sit on my finger and bop your head up and down. We always had fun together no matter what. Thank you. I remember the many times you hung out on my shoulder around the house, the two of us just being happy together.

I remember the time when we lived in Queens Village and Portia and I were doing a spiritual exercise; my eyes were closed. We were sitting in front of each other, and she said, "What do you see?"

I said I saw green in my heart area, and your little voice sounded off loudly at the same time. Portia said she saw you in my heart, wings wide open. It was such a powerful exercise, and you were right there doing it with us. Thank you!

You are in my heart. I remember when I was at my mom's house once and you were on my shoulder. She reached over to give me a kiss on the cheek, and you bit her. Your possessiveness was somewhat charming. Thank you! You always had a spunky attitude, cautious about letting people get close to us.

I remember when we lived at Idlewild, and you got out of bed, walking on the floor and yelling at us because we were being loud, disturbing your sleep.

I loved the many times when you finished your food and then threw down your bowl on the floor to let me know you were done. And the maid came over and cleaned it up. You should see the mess Petey is making now. We are going to need two maids with him, and there is only one of me!

It took you a while to warm up to Babe. I recall for a long time you'd bite him, and in the last couple years, it seems like you grew to love him so much. You started squeaking and flying back and forth when he pulled up in the driveway and beeped his horn. It seems like you never settled down unless he came over and scratched you. Thank you for loving him so deeply, and I am sorry if you did not understand why he was no longer in our lives.

I want to thank you for loving Carol when you stayed with her. Thank you for letting Leslie take care of you when we were in New York. Thank you for loving Maureen and letting her take care of you when I traveled for work a lot. Thank you for loving Christine and letting her care for you. Thank you for loving Shawn and Matt and for choosing to leave this planet when they were here because you knew they would be here to love and support me through this very difficult time. Thank you for the way you snuggled up in Matt's hand and fell asleep and gave him kisses the night before you passed. Thank you for letting Shawn pet you and give you head rubs on that night. Thank you for the way you loved Marie over the years and for doing EFT with us week after week when she came over every week during that year. I want you to know that Brenda adored you, and she even talked her friend into getting a conure because you are so sweet. Thank you for getting to know Marianne and Lynn. Thank you for letting Tiffany and Kirk care for you and for loving Radar. The way you and Radar were with each other was just the cutest thing ever. I wish I had a picture.

I thought about you every day before. Now I think about you every minute, and I hope I gave you a full life and all the happiness you deserved. The last few months have been tough. I know the biweekly baths were uncomfortable for you. I am so sorry if I hurt you, my love. I hope I was as gentle with you in your pain as you have been gentle with me through my painful experiences. Thank you for your gentleness.

I never imagined you wouldn't be in my life and I refused to see all the signs.

I love you always,

Mommy

January 15, 2018

The statue of Saint Francis arrived on Saturday, and I placed it in the backyard where Pepper is buried. I filled the birdbath attached to it with water and planted yellow and purple tulips in front of the area where she is buried. I look out the French doors of my living room observing this in silence. I looked at the dark circles under my eyes this morning. I don't understand why I have dark circles. It seems like I've slept at least fourteen hours a couple nights this week.

I get Petey covered for bed, and then I become overwhelmed with emptiness and the loss of Pepper. I go to bed, hoping to sleep it off. This morning was the first day I meditated at home in the past week. I just saw some blue jays outside the kitchen window. They are calling. One was sitting on the plumeria, and he looked me in the eyes and had a lot to say. Pepper, I know you are sending me a message that everything is fine, and you are here. Hello sweet girl.

I woke up last night and read an email from Louise. I met Louise at the Community of Mindfulness center at the Beginning Anew ceremony on New Year's Eve. In her email she quoted a message from Thich Nhat Hanh. The message has brought me to a place of peace because I know it's true. Louise wrote:

> Oh, Karen, I'm so sorry to hear of your loss. This reminds me of a scene in the film *Walk with Me* (about life in Plum Village), where Thich Nhat Hanh offers comfort to a child who has expressed great sadness upon the dying of her dog. I can't remember exactly what he said to her, but it's along these lines:
>
>> It's like a cloud in the sky. When the cloud is no longer in the sky, it doesn't mean the cloud has died. The cloud is continued in other forms like rain or snow or ice. So, you can recognize your cloud in her new forms. If you are very fond of a beautiful cloud and if your cloud is no longer there, you should not be sad. Your beloved cloud might have become the rain, calling on you, "Darling, darling, don't you see me in my new form?" And then you will not be stuck with grief and despair. Your beloved one continues always.

Meditation helps you recognize her continued presence in new forms. And our nature is the nature of no birth and no death … the nature of a cloud also. A cloud can never die. A cloud can become snow, or hail … or rain. But it is impossible for a cloud to pass from being into non-being. And that is true with your beloved one. She has not died. She is continued in many new forms. And you can look deeply and recognize herself in you and around you.

Knowing this, I am at peace *now*.

January 16, 2018

In a dream this morning, I was lying in the bed on my left side with my right leg resting on top of my left leg, elevated to allow my left hip to rest comfortably flat. The right side of my body and right shoulder was up off the bed slightly. In the dream, Pepper was cuddled up between the upper left and middle of my chest. She was cozy and turned her head slightly and looked me in the eyes. The awareness entered my mind that I may crush her, so I lifted my right hand and petted her, checking whether she was okay. She fluffed up her feathers to let me know she was happy and comfy. She moved in and rubbed her head on my chin. I felt so much joy, and she smiled at me. In my dream, I had the awareness that I was dreaming, and my body was in that exact position. I woke up and I was lying in that position. I smiled big.

Chapter 5

Escaping

....

There is a kind of radio in our minds called NST, Non-Stop Thinking. We have to turn off that kind of radio in order to feel connected to life. If we aren't aware of our thoughts, they run rampant through our mind and take up residence there. They don't wait for an invitation.

—Thich Nhat Hanh, *Silence*

January 25, 2018

Losing Pepper has been like losing my anchor. I'm floating out at sea with no direction or purpose. I realize that she was the energy that grounded me for the last nineteen years. The last couple of weeks have been very intense. This is the worst I've felt in my life. There is this huge hole in our home and inside of me. In the last couple of weeks, my evenings have consisted of putting Petey to bed and then going to bed to escape the emotions that were coming up inside of me. It often felt like there was a ton of bricks lying on my chest. I've been sleeping fourteen hours at a time. I have completely lost my appetite. I'm not been able to socialize much, and I am afraid to leave the house mostly because I am worried about Petey. Petey has been following me around from room to room, and when he cannot see me, he screams continuously. He has followed me into the bathroom and sat on the window curtain rod until I was done showering. His chirps are long, sharp, and distressed the whole time. But if I talk to him while showering, it calms him down. I've had sudden outbursts of crying, especially when driving and when I think of the way Pepper looked at me with so much love.

I finally went to my doctor and asked to have a short-term antidepressant to help with the intensity of the grief I am experiencing. The protocol was to take one a day for three days and then twice a day, and I think today it finally kicked in. I started painting a picture of Pepper. I woke up last night and completed a chapter in the other book I am working on. It feels like I am trying to fill the emptiness, and I could just be with it and allow it because it is not going to kill me. I have reached out to other pet lovers to console me and especially because I needed comforting. I am receiving comfort and support from my closest friends. Marie checks on me every day.

Today as I was driving Petey to the vet, I became aware that I am not awake. I am either focusing on memories of Pepper and being upset or trying to escape by looking for something to become attached to. I noticed my thoughts running over fantasies just to escape the tightness in my chest. I started to consciously name the things I was seeing in front of me. That traffic light is red. As I stared at it, I focused on my breathing in and out, and it helped to calm the chatter of my mind. I also noticed the intensity of the red light. As I continued driving, I named as many things as possible.

The vet who saw Petey took me into a room, and we discussed Pepper. She was very fond of Pepper and had met Pepper for the first time when I'd brought her in for what we thought was a broken wing. It was a benign tumor. She explained that the biopsy they had taken of Pepper's uropygial gland was inconclusive and the Vets avoided getting additional samples because Pepper was not doing well under the anesthesia. She explained that, although the biopsy was negative there was something going on in her uropygial gland. She thinks it may have been cancer that spread to the rest of her body, and the only treatments they would have been able to give to Pepper would have been administered under anesthesia. Since she did not do well under anesthesia, her chances of surviving would've diminished. The vet spent a long time explaining, and she assured me there was nothing else I could have done to save her. She complimented me for being so consistent with bringing Pepper and Petey in for visits. She reassured me that Pepper was lucky to have had such a long life and had been well taken care of. We know she was at least nineteen, and when I got her, I was told she was five. She was at least twenty-four years old—maybe.

I felt at peace leaving the vet's office. I came home and started on a painting of Pepper. I am now shifting my perspective to cherishing the wonderful moments we had and the love that we shared.

Today, I have an awareness that the things that are going on in my mind are disrupting my state of peace. These images of the past are wonderful. I've lived them. I am now in this new moment, and it's okay to recall good memories and to accept and nurture the pain inside me until the pain subsides. Most importantly, I know that healing occurs gradually, and I am patient and kind with myself in the process. Awareness guides me back to being the observer of my thoughts and emotions. The choice to be in awareness is my escape from the sea of thoughts that somehow drudge up sadness and leave me stuck in pain.

In contrast, I am also aware of the times when I look to others to escape the pain I am experiencing. The choice to bring awareness to as many moments as possible helps me to awake fully to my current reality. The choice to observe events and circumstances occurring with a sense of detachment is very freeing. By doing so, my identity is no longer connected to the labels attached to my personality. Instead, I am just being. Being! Yes, I am just being aware.

As I am waking up to my present reality, I first notice how many times I become caught up in the stories in my mind. I can experience life fully if I am aware of what is happening in front of me moment by moment. I can only accomplish this if I am in the moment as it occurs. I become engulfed in a memory, my awareness of the thoughts related to that memory and the things that triggered those thoughts allow me to bring myself back to the reality in front of me. This also brings awareness to the emotions I am experiencing and sheds awareness on associated thoughts with the intent of accepting that these are thoughts. This is not what is happening in my reality in front of me. The memory is a recollection of what has already happened. As I accept my thoughts as thoughts, I tune into the way I feel in my body and the emotions that are surfacing as a result of the thoughts I am having. I choose to allow my thoughts to pass by without fighting, judging or attaching to them. I simply acknowledge them as my thoughts. This is not what is happening in my reality in front of me. The memory is a recollection of what has already happened. As I accept my thoughts as thoughts, I tune into the way I feel in my body and the emotions that are surfacing as a result of the thoughts I am having. I choose to allow my thoughts to pass by without fighting, judging or attaching to them. I simply acknowledge them as my thoughts.

By doing so, slowly, I break the pattern by noticing how often I have the thoughts—just noticing. When I do, I bring myself back to my breath and to naming the things in front of me. I need not struggle with my thoughts. I accept that they are there and remind myself that what is in front of me is what is my reality. As the same thoughts come up over and over, I investigate the nature of these thoughts and what in me is causing them. The discomfort always comes from within me. In doing so, I am accepting responsibility for my thoughts and the way I choose to interpret and view my own existence. The thoughts that result in afflicted emotions such as fear, sadness, grief, anxiety, shame, or guilt are especially important.

When I struggle or try to escape from thoughts as they come up, I bring awareness to my condition as it is. I am being with my experience. Breathing through the discomfort, I know that this too will pass. This is not going to kill me. Breathing into the space in the center of my chest and recognizing that I can be with difficult emotions fully calms my emotional state and restores my peace. This also allows the emotion to pass through me and move out of my energy field.

I believe emotions are energy in motion. When I am experiencing one of the heavier emotions, breathing deeply while allowing it brings awareness to what is happening right now. By focusing my awareness on where the emotion is arising in my body, I can allow the emotions to *be* in my space without resistance. There is great power in *allowing*. When I allow myself to be fully present with the emotion in my present moment experience, I ultimately set the stage to allow the emotion to pass through my energy field.

Shifting emotional states comes with pausing to acknowledge what is coming up inside of me and then bringing my full awareness to the matter. Some helpful things I do when struggling with sadness, for example, is to notice where it is in my body. When the sadness is overwhelming, and I am unable to shake it, I sit quietly with it and breathe into the emotion. Sometimes heart-focused breathing is effective. I am a Certified Heartmath Coach(a science based certification to help access the power and intelligence of the heart) and have found that breathing into my heart is one of the most effective ways to get out of my head and into my heart. The Heartmath Institute have developed ways to deal with stress and increase resilience. There are so many other benefits. By allowing emotions to surface without resistance, I accept that these emotions are in me and passing through me. I am more aware that I am not my emotions, and therefore, they don't control me. I am experiencing emotions. Once I can sit with a heavy emotion and experience it, I am able to be gentle and compassionate with myself until the emotion no longer overwhelms me.

It's vital to being in my reality. Not escaping into the stories or fantasies in my mind is my goal after all!

What I experience with my senses is real. The keys on this keyboard are real. The computer monitor is real. As I expand my awareness of my life experience, I am more aware that I unconsciously escape into my stories. Becoming more aware of the stories that play out in my mind empowers me to choose to take the necessary steps to bring myself back to what is reality in this moment right now. By being more present and mindful in my life experience, I am *living*. I am *living awake*.

Although I have so many memories with Pepper, I know there are so many moments I missed because I wasn't fully present in my experience, doing one thing at a time. So now I am fully present with Petey, and he is becoming closer to me because we sit together for an hour in the evening. I look at him when he is eating, he looks at me, and we experience life together, moment by moment.

Today I accept that I have been escaping life by constantly listening to the chatter in my mind and living in my fantasies to escape what is in front of me. When I choose to be in my experience fully, I am allowing myself to create my life from the reality that is in front of me. I am experiencing what is right here, right now. Training myself to be here and not in my mind is what will enable me to be here in this present moment and experience it fully.

As I was painting, I felt the most present I have been in the last two weeks. I looked at the colors and mixed the colors to perfection. I spent the last couple days sketching Pepper on the canvas, delightfully noticing her flexibility and her beauty in the posture she was in. I found myself going back and forth until I could see that the picture I drew was a true depiction of the picture I was painting. I paid attention to every detail. The picture was taken in 2006. Pepper was only twelve years old. She is glowing, healthy, and flexible, and it is wonderful to paint this picture because it imprints a positive memory of her in perfect health.

Painting of Pepper

Chapter 6

Returning

....

Whether you think you can or you think you can't, you're right.

—Henry Ford

March 9, 2018

It's been a while since I've written. In the meantime, so much has transpired in my life. Back in October, I wanted to explore going back to school to attain my PhD in philosophy. My first step was to sign up for the GRE class. I picked the next available online class, which started on February and was scheduled from 7:00 to 10:00 p.m. every Tuesday and Thursday for a month. I spent at least twelve additional hours a week refreshing myself on basic math, algebra, geometry, statistics, exponents, and so on—it was brutal.

After the class ended, I planned on spending the following two months studying every Tuesday and Thursday from 7:00 to 10:00 p.m. as if I was in class, with the intention of scheduling the GRE exam in May. While at my appointment with my therapist Ann today, I expressed that I was overwhelmed. She advised that I needed to give myself a break and breathe. Do this from March through July. Put things on my social calendar and take a day off so I could go connect with Mother Earth. Most importantly, I should focus on the frequency that I want to be in. She said, "Be selfish about the frequency of your body."

I felt a sense of relief. I gave myself permission to stop. Ann mentioned that I needed to do all the things I really enjoy. So here I am writing again. Let me catch you up! After my class started, I had my first session with Ann on February 19. Prior to that, she'd offered me a complimentary phone session. I shared about my life, and Ann mentioned that she utilizes art therapy, which would help me with the grieving process. I mentioned on our call that I'd decided to have no contact with my ex.

The first in-person session was focused around grieving Pepper. However, Ann mentioned that my grief was compounded and that I was grieving my failed marriage, as well as the loss of the adoption and possibly my only chance to be a parent as well. We looked at the beliefs, thoughts, and behaviors I'd developed as a child—as well as an adult. We did art around the grieving process.

For homework, Ann gave me the book *The Seven Principles for Making Marriage Work* by John M. Gottman PhD, and my other homework was to write ten non-negotiables that I desired in a partner. When I left Ann's office that day, I committed to texting one final text to inform my ex that I was not going to be in touch with him and would be blocking his number. This also meant breaking ties with his friends. The attachment identified in my session, to "not being rejected," played out immediately in my behavior. I paid attention to what was going on inside of me, feeling my emotions and observing the nature of my thoughts and my reactions.

Before I share what happened next, I want to share that I am a member of the local Community of Mindfulness. However, I am not Buddhist.

After my therapy session on February 19 at 6:30 p.m., I started an intensive at the mindfulness center, "Mindful Practices for Emotional Healing."

The first call outlined expectations of the course:

- Practice daily meditation sitting in the morning for thirty minutes (piece of cake!)
- Take meditation breaks throughout the day (might be challenging when I was working in the office, but possible on my work from home days)

- Take inventory by logging date/time, circumstances/situations, what emotional suffering was present, how it felt/manifested in the body, what thoughts were present, and whether there was a story or theme (seemed intense)
- Read the book *Emotional Alchemy* by Tara Bennett-Goleman
- Read the book *A New Earth* by Eckhart Tolle

In addition, we would have a mentoring call, as well as a separate in-person group session held biweekly. My in-person group sessions were on Sundays after *sangha* at the center.

At our first peer group meeting on February 25, I didn't expect to share as much as I did. But it just came out, and so too did the tears. We all shared what was going on in our lives and what had prompted us to take the intensive. It felt like such a safe space to share. This center has been that for me.

The previous day had been spent lying on the couch feeling the heaviness in my chest and knowing that I had homework to read two books and piles of GRE homework, and yet I could not get off the couch. I allowed myself to feel the intensity of the heaviness in my chest and gut, and I stayed with it until it passed. As a matter of fact, this heaviness had been in my being all week and as I was logging my emotions.

I started noticing a pattern that had been a theme throughout my life. I realized I'd been playing the same tapes over and over my entire life—sadness! It also seemed like the recent events occurring in my life had a compounded effect of grief, and as a result I found myself bursting out into tears unexpectedly and uncontrollably.

After sangha the previous week, we gathered for tea. A member at the mindfulness center asked me what was going on in my life. Out of nowhere, I started crying and could not control myself, and I was not able to get the words out. It was also in the middle of a room where others were socializing. I was embarrassed, and yet this individual held the space for me to feel safe.

I got home that Sunday, and out of nowhere, there was so much resistance coming up inside of me—thoughts like, *This reality stuff is too real for me*, and, *Being present and mindful is so intense*. My ego sneaked in, and immediately I began thinking about the alternatives to digging up all this stuff on top of already having so many life events lately.

I *thought* about my alternatives some more, and suddenly I had reasons coming out of thin air as to why this journey I was on to awaken to reality was a waste of time. All this talk about suffering felt too heavy. How did we know that the Buddha was right? Had anyone fact-checked the Buddha? I thought I could choose to go through this life experience totally unawake, living in the past or future, and it would never really matter because "form is emptiness" and there is "no thing."

And it continued. *I don't believe in an afterlife, so it's not like I'm ever going to come back here. And no matter (the thing that everything is made of) matters anyway!* I was coming up with more reasons to escape.

At the end of the night, I decided that maybe I wasn't going to go back to the mindfulness center, and since I needed some positivity to hold on to, I recorded myself reading some treatments from the book *The Science of Mind* by Ernest Holmes. Specifically, I recorded, "A Treatment to Heal Confusion and Discord," "I Am Not Bound by Any Mistake," and "My Ideal Merges into the Real." I also recorded myself reading Louise Hay's "Love Treatment" from her book *You Can Heal Your Life*. I listened to those over and over that night and the next day while I worked. Things felt lighter in my being.

After work the next day, I lay on the couch and waited to see if Petey would come sit on me. It's mandatory that I spend at least an hour on the couch with him daily. As I lay down on the couch, a memory of Pepper came into my mind. I thought of her walking across my chest during the last days of her life when we lay together on the couch in the evening. I saw myself petting her head and neck feathers as she walked across my chest and looked into my eyes. I thought to myself, *I wonder why I don't have a lot of more specific memories with Pepper.*

And then my next thought was, *It's because I wasn't always completely present with her. I was always doing something else.*

My next thought was, *I need to be more present with Petey, so I don't miss out on moments with him. This way, I can remember every minute with him."* Or at least I can try to.

As I was thinking these thoughts, Petey was making his way over to the top of my toe where my feet were crossed. My hands were tucked under the blanket since I'd noticed that he didn't come near me if my hands were out. He didn't want to be touched—not by me. I had logged it in my emotional log as "frustration." There is a picture included here of him sitting on me the way he likes to. I looked at him, and he fluffed up his feathers around his cheeks and his chin area. This meant he was happy. In that moment, I saw an impression of the Buddhist monk Bodhidharma in Petey's expression.

Hmmmmm.

My next thought was, *Bodhidharma reincarnated into my bird to teach me to be present,* followed by, *And Pepper was here to teach me what unconditional love looks like.*

I was introduced to Bodhidharma at the silent retreat when a scroll of him was up on the wall in front of the meditation hall at the retreat. I found myself doing my meditation with open eyes for the first time while looking directly into Bodhidharma's eyes. I noticed that the meditation was the most spacious meditation I'd experienced. It was so powerful for me that, after the retreat, I ordered a scroll of Bodhidharma, framed it, and hung it above my meditation mat. I usually meditate with eyes closed. However, just having that scroll in my room after that experience has made me more at ease.

I looked into Petey's eyes, totally present with him as he kept his gaze focused, looking into my eyes. I began to feel completely still within my being. I heard my breathing, and the sound of my heartbeat was prominent. Soon, it seemed liked everything around me was not there. The two of us were breathing in and out, absorbed in the moment, looking into each other's eyes. I felt like time stopped. There were no thoughts for maybe five minutes.

Something happened inside of me where there was an increase of energy moving. I felt it in my midsection from my hips all the way to my brain. It was like the movement of energy up the legs or through the arms to the fingertips that I'd experienced in some yoga poses—except the intensity was at least 75 percent greater, and that is just a guess (if I had to put a number to it). My point is that the energy I felt was significantly larger than that I'd experienced being in a yoga pose. There was so much energy that my midsection and legs were drenched in sweat. My entire midsection felt like it had opened down the middle. My ears felt like the holes were expanding, and I felt a sensation in the center of my brain that was illuminating and sparkly.

I also felt like I'd shifted from my reality that I normally experienced into a different space. This space was continuous, and time stopped. It felt like I was in eternity, and there was an overwhelming presence about it. I heard myself breathing louder and more clearly. My focus was just to be completely absorbed with Petey, and he never flinched. He looked at me intently.

When my mind crept back in, the first thought I had was, *I only see time as a reality because I'm existing in mind. There is no time and I am 100 percent certain of it.*

After putting Petey to bed that night, I wrote this experience down in my log and expressed that "reality rules!"

March 6, 2018

I listened to the recorded forum for the intensive that I'd missed while away visiting Portia in Pennsylvania the previous weekend. Fred stated:

In areas of my life I have suffering, have I really acknowledged it. There are parts of me that are suffering or in areas of my life I am suffering. Parts of me are still reacting emotionally and behaviorally and there is a point where you are done with it.

Do I really want to be emotionally whole?

Can I really be free of it? Am I just paying lip service?

Do I really want to end my suffering?

It felt like he was speaking specifically to me. He continued to invite us to believe in the efficacy of the training or teaching. He said:

When you acknowledge your suffering, believe you can be whole emotionally, then you will get well. Acknowledge you have found a methodology that works. Begin by learning how to be present with yourself and be present to mind states that are unpleasant. The presence of resistance tells you that you are stuck. You don't have to be overwhelmed by it. Be aware of what is arising and just hold it in awareness. The reality cannot change, but the way I relate is my freedom. There is your freedom. This is the reality of my life! How can I relate to the reality of it that is most beneficial to me? That changes the conversation within me. People suffer because they constantly ruminate about past situations or people suffer because of the future because they constantly fantasize about negative outcomes. There is another way ... and you're beginning to learn it. It's going to take time ... until you have your own experience with this where you have begun to see that your capacity to change and transform is real, that you can do it. In the beginning you can actually rely on your elders.

Then he said later in the forum while speaking to the topic of afflicted emotions, "It's my sadness looking for something to be sad about."

How did I luck out in finding such a great teacher who is a disciple of Thich Nhat Hanh in the same city that I live in, who always sums up and addresses all my crap? Poignant. I must remember as I am breathing in and out that freedom is not my reality. Freedom is how I relate to each moment.

March 16, 2018

I turned on the TV, and on the scientific channel there was a tribute to Stephen Hawking, who'd passed away a couple days earlier. He was speaking to the meaning of life. Since I was age ten when I started meditating, I had a deep yearning to understand what the meaning of life is. I had searched and read tons of books and gotten involved in many different disciplines because I needed to understand what the meaning of life is. In the tribute, it was noted that Stephen Hawking said, "The meaning of life is the meaning that you give it."

This resonates as truth for me. I finally got my answer, and I am honored to have been alive while Stephen Hawking was here on this planet. I choose the meaning I give life going forward, and that is practicing being here in my body experiencing life daily. Being present in the day-to-day reality of my existence is my top priority. The gift is the newness of each day and the understanding that I always have the power of choice.

I can choose to be with my experience fully. I can choose to be with my emotions and not be reactive to them. I am empowered to accept everything as it is and be with discomfort when it arises. It's not going to kill me. I see things differently, knowing that I survived divorce (twice), death, failed opportunity to be a parent, the fear of my dad dying, rejection, and all the other stuff that I've ever felt terrified by. I survived, and I am here now. It's up to me to be here experiencing the rest of my life each day and to be okay with whatever that is. I am empowered to do that! Understanding that I have a choice in every moment to be free of the prison of thoughts that plague me every moment of the day is what gives me my conviction to make the rest of my life experience amazing.

First, I am simply bringing awareness to my breath. By being aware of my breathing, I can exist in my body and not in my mind. By doing so, I solidify the reality I experience with my senses—not the one in my mind. By doing so, I accept and embrace my experience of life.

March 30, 2018

I've been having more present and mindful moments in the past two weeks. After hearing Fred's forum, I decided that I was no longer going to be sad. I am tired of bumbling through life being sad about everything that has already happened. I am tired of dwelling and ruminating. I'm done!

I've started having a greater awareness of the quality of the feeling of sadness when it creeps into my body—that slight heaviness in my chest and/or gut. Then by being able to feel the feeling as soon as it is coming on, I can have an awareness of the thoughts that occurred prior to the feeling coming up in my body. Next, I stop and be still for a minute. I breathe into this feeling and really feel it without engaging in the thoughts that triggered the feeling. By doing this in the past weeks, I have slowly exiled sadness out of my life.

The homework assigned for the last couple weeks was to read chapters 5 and 6 of *A New Earth*, which talks about the pain body. I can relate to the feeling of being sick and tired of the same afflictive emotions triggering me all the time. It's my choice not to be hijacked by my thoughts and emotions anymore. I am not doing it. And once I had the realization that this can be a choice, I no longer felt trapped. I still have and probably will always have moments of sadness, but I am certain that it is not going to be my identity anymore. I am not going to live my life being sad and pathetic.

Chapter 7

Accepting Impermanence

....

*It is real and deep wisdom to learn to look
at things in terms of manifestation. If someone
who is very close to you has passed away and you define
him or her as non-existing, you are mistaken. From
nothing cannot be born something...
If you look deeply, you can touch his or her presence
in other forms of manifestation.*

—Thich Nhat Hanh, *No Death, No Fear*

April 9, 2018

Lately, I wake up each day affirming, "Today is a new day, twenty-four hours ahead of me. I vow to live this day in mindfulness, seeing everything with the eyes of compassion." Today I woke up around 4:00 a.m. I lay in bed meditating until 5:30 a.m. My meditations are spent sitting or lying with eyes closed in silence. I am consciously breathing. My in breath and out breath come and go like waves. My awareness is heightened. I am the observer of my mind. Thoughts come and go. My goal is to stay in the space of awareness, just being the observer of my thoughts without following them or becoming caught up in them. Often, I realize I am thinking after I have been caught up in a story or a wish. I come back to stillness. I accept without judgment that it is the nature of my mind to wander in thought. I breathe in and out deeply, consciously. I bring myself back to focusing on the wave of in and out breathing. I continue to be the observer of what arises in my mind. I am patient. I allow myself to experience the stillness of the space between thoughts. The more I do this, the greater my desire is to experience silence and stillness in my day. This is my true anchor—the cord that connects me to everything in the universe.

Lately, it is in this space that I open to understanding the nature of impermanence. Impermanence is the changing nature of everything. It is the acceptance of the wavelike pattern of my breath—my life force. Impermanence is also the nature of mind to think and the observance of how thoughts come and go. It is the observance of emotions that come up in my body as thoughts arise. By allowing myself to be still enough to flow with this current, I am acquiring a deeper understanding of the nature of my existence. I can see clearly that these are all aspects of the expression of me as human. I am life expressing through me. My physical body as I know it is the vessel through which life expresses. My thoughts are mental energy. My life is the expression of this mental energy. All these aspects of myself are as impermanent as the in and out breath that give me life. The breath changes. I observe, and I notice that there is a space following my in breath, and then comes the out breath.

In my meditation I continue being the observer, and this goes on for some time. At some point, I get the insight to go back to chapter 2 and add, "I am nothing, and I am everything," where I mention that I have not had the courage to be honest about not being Christian. I am still. It occurs to me that I've been aware that this chapter on impermanence needed to be written next, and the resistance I feel has been stemming from associating accepting impermanence with accepting death. I receive insight that, by declaring this statement every day upon awakening—Today is a new day, twenty-four hours ahead of me. I vow to live this day in mindfulness seeing everything with the eyes of compassion—I am accepting that every moment ahead of me today is new and different and, therefore, changing. This is truly where I need to start as I aspire to accept the nature of existence as impermanence.

And suddenly, all the fear I've been having around writing about accepting impermanence releases its grip on me. I realize that the only goal I need to have is to welcome each moment as fresh and new and to strive to be fully aware in every moment. In doing so, I am allowing myself to be free from the fear of something ending. I am being with the beginning and ending of each moment, and therefore, I can accept the impermanence of it. There is no struggle when I see each moment as a cycle of birth and death, each breath as a cycle of birth and death. In this way, each thought is a cycle of birth and death. Each day is a cycle of birth and death. Each season is a cycle of birth and death. Each expression of life, whether it be human, plant, or animal, is a cycle of birth and death.

Coming out of my meditation, I still question why I'm overwhelmed by the fear of losing my dad. Even though Pepper is speaking to me through the birds outside my window and in the backyard daily, I wonder why I still hurt so deeply when I think that I will never hear her voice again or be able to touch her. Why do I miss her so much? I understand the nature of impermanence. I know we are all going to die. I know that death is part of the cycle of life.

Understanding the concept of impermanence is important. However, while knowing something on an intellectual level brings understanding, wisdom and humbleness, there is still the experiential pain of loss as the emotional world lives in a different realm. To me this is like the idea of reading about the quality of an apple—let's say a red delicious apple. It is red and has a certain shape and contains vitamins and minerals and is better for my body than eating potato chips. If I've never eaten an apple, I really have only learned what it is by understanding the theoretical or conceptual description or a basic explanation of what this apple is. However, when I eat an apple, I have an experience with it. From this experience, I learn that, when I bite into an apple, taste the sweetness, and become familiar with the texture of it—when I eat the apple—I have experienced it. It is now a part of who I am. I also see that it is white on the inside and has seeds at its core. My concept of the apple changes from a theoretical understanding to an experiential understanding of the quality of having an apple. As a result of this experience, I know what it is like to have an apple. It leaves an imprint in my memory, and going forward, I can recall what the various qualities of this fruit are. Then I can decide if I like it or not and whether I am going to eat it again.

Our loved ones are the most valuable imprints in our memories. We become attached to these imprints. When they are gone, the memory still lives on inside us. This is not a bad thing or a good thing. Losing someone we love creates an opening inside of us, allowing deeper understanding. And there is a "grieving process" as they call it. We honor that process because it's our way of letting go slowly and accepting that we will no longer have the loved one in that form that we once knew them in.

I've chosen to hold onto the words in the book *No Death, No Fear* by Thich Nhat Hanh as my comfort, and this has been powerful for me as I come to terms with the loss of Pepper in the physical form. I find it easy and effortless to bring myself back when I am overwhelmed by focusing on my breathing and repeating the affirmations below:

> Breathing in, I contemplate letting go
> Breathing out, I experience the joy of letting go
> or
> Breathing in I am accepting and allowing
> Breathing out I am letting go (Thich Nhat Hanh)

The lesson I have learned from Pepper passing unexpectedly is to really be fully present with the people whom I love and are closest to me. As this presence increases, it will become more natural to be present with everyone. It made me see that the best gift I can give to anyone I love is my *presence* and my willingness to listen deeply to whatever the person is sharing without the need to give advice or share my views. I know Pepper loved me unconditionally, and it is now my duty to be the expression of the unconditional love that she taught me by being able to really listen, understand, and remember what has been shared with me by others. It's important for me to look people in the eyes when they are speaking with me and not be distracted. These small things are the way I am shifting my reality to my current reality. It's also important for me to make an effort to remember names and to address people by their names. I am aspiring to listen deeply without interrupting. I am committing to having a sense of curiosity about the people closest to me, asking questions, and trying to recall important details about what matters to them.

It's important for me to honor the way I process loss and allow myself to be with it and not rush it or drag it out. I need to have awareness of myself and to breathe in and out deeply when emotions are heavy or the moments are difficult. It's important to honor the transformative process of energy and honor Pepper (and anyone else who passes) by listening to the birds chirping outside in the morning and spending a few minutes to really take it all in. Spending time in nature also keeps me connected with the cycles of life and the awareness that, even though there is birth and death, there is always beauty, and beauty may express itself in the form of flowers, such as the orchids or birds of paradise in my yard. It also expresses in the form of the caterpillars and grasshoppers who nibble on the leaves of my veggies growing in the garden. I am aware of everything around me in nature. I am aware of the clouds in the sky and the nature with which they shift and change. I am aware of the cycle of birth and death of the grass that grows in my yard. I am aware of the cycle of birth and death of the waves as I observe the waves come in and recede as I take walks on the beach.

The nature of impermanence is that everything is changing. This is happening whether I choose to be a part of it and accept it or not. When the choice is mine to flow with the currents of life, there is no struggle. I am choosing to flow with the currents of life, breathing in an out and knowing that the only thing that is constant is change and that the only thing that will be unchanged is the space between the cycles of everything. This space, this stillness, is the underlying current that binds all of existence. Knowing this, I choose to be with change. I am naturally calm and at ease in my being.

I saw this clearly through the monastics who were guest speakers at the mindfulness center yesterday. There was calmness and ease in their expressions. They truly walk the talk as you would say. As questions were asked of them, each person answered the exact question that was asked and then answered the questions that had been asked previously. They were truly paying attention and listening deeply—fully here and in the moment. Seeing this example, I am more committed to practicing mindfulness of my breath, my thoughts, and my emotions, no matter what I am doing. With consistent practice, my awareness increases. I am living the reality in front of me.

As I observe my thoughts and emotions when they come up, I breathe in and out, accepting that I am not my thoughts or emotions. I am simply experiencing them, and thoughts and emotions are also in a constant state of flux within me. They move in and out through me and there is no need to struggle or resist any thought or emotion. Simply understanding their impermanent nature and being the observer of the thoughts and emotions allows them to move in and out, flowing freely. Breathing consciously when heavier emotions come up allows me to create space within myself—for the energy I am experiencing to flow freely without grasping on or getting stuck in my body.

Chapter 8

Discovering

· ·

For every action, there is an equal and opposite reaction.
—Isaac Newton (Newton's third law of motion)

April 10, 2018

I am becoming more aware of the un-storied "self" inside of me. In my meditation this morning, I experienced more of my true self. There are bigger pauses between the flood of thoughts. I am also feeling calmer throughout my days because I am more conscious of my breathing. When I realize that I am lost in thought, I gently bring myself back to my in breath and my out breath. Then I refocus on what is in front of me. I refocus on reality.

My senses are heightened. I was able to lie on the couch with eyes closed and identify the types of birds that are eating from the bird feeder hung on the oak tree outside my back door. I listened and identified each type of bird by the sound it makes. Earlier today, I identified woodpeckers. Then later, I heard the cardinals out there. I also know when the morning doves are on the ground feeding and become spooked. The flutter of their wings is distinct and only morning doves have that specific vibration when they flap their wings.

I also notice when the mockingbirds sit outside the kitchen window on the hedge and look directly into the kitchen. There is usually only one at a time, and the bird chirps nonstop until I go over to the kitchen window and make eye contact with it. We look into each other's eyes for a while, and it usually continues chirping for a minute or two and then takes off. I usually say, "Hi, Pepper. I know you're here, sweetheart."

I don't feed the birds in the front yard, and I can't come up with any good reason why these birds insist on getting my attention when they are on the hedge while I am in the kitchen.

April 25, 2018

I was wondering in the past week why I keep logging the dates when I write and it occurred to me that I've been compelled to share the dates of my writing because I am processing life in the present moment and sharing about the practical aspect of being mindful. There are wonderful teachers with extravagant "how-tos" on the subject. Truthfully speaking, being present and completely mindful, in my experience, is the most difficult objective I've set out to do. I believe it's because thought waves are of a higher frequency than matter. This could be why I'm continually drawn to my thoughts. I'm certain that there are scientific explanations regarding various frequencies as it relates to thoughts, as well as matter.

I linger onto my childhood because I was so devoted as a Catholic. I prayed the rosary. I believed so deeply. Then around age ten, I started practicing meditation with my friend Merlin, who is Hindu. I began questioning everything. Blind faith was no longer part of me. While growing up in Trinidad, I attended the Roman Catholic Church every Sunday morning.

I have always felt very connected to the saints—some more than others. Saint Francis is my favorite because of his undying commitment to his faith, kind heart, and love of all people and animals. I am closest to and call on Saint Michael (Archangel Michael) for protection. I have Archangel Michael cards and a wooden carving of Saint Michael because he has been my personal protector. I often say, "Archangel Michael, please put your shield around me." I feel like he is with me, and his shield and energy engulf and protect me. If I lose something or am looking for something that I've misplaced, I ask Saint Anthony to help me find said item, and shortly thereafter, I find it. It is easy to feel the energy of the saints around me. This is probably because they walked the earth.

As a child, I attended St. Patrick Catholic Church while growing up in Trinidad. It just so happens that there is a St. Patricks' Church about two minutes from my house. I wondered if this was a coincidence. Maybe! I have never attended this church. Over the years, when I've gone to a Catholic church, I've been reminded of my childhood, and there is a nostalgic feeling that's part of the imprint of who I am.

I attended my third silent retreat between April 19, 2018, and April 22, 2018. These retreats are held at the Franciscan Retreat Center located on the Hillsborough River. It is beautiful there. My first silent retreat was in April 2017, and at that time, I just happened to be reading *Saint Francis* by Nikos Kazantzakis. I picked it up after reading about Saint Francis in one of Wayne Dyer's books. I felt drawn to Saint Francis. When I purchased the book in December 2016, there were only used copies and maybe just two. I felt strongly about reading this book and decided to purchase the copy that was not marked up and in good condition. I didn't want to purchase a book that was highlighted and underlined, because I underline and highlight more than I don't in books; it's just how I have always read. I would be distracted by reading someone else's book that was totally marked up. I couldn't put the book down, and surprisingly, I did not underline or highlight a single thing.

While I was in the middle of the book, out of the blue, I received an email from the mindfulness center inviting nonmembers to join in a silent retreat at the Franciscan Center. I *knew* I had to be there. I signed up immediately and shared the info with my friend Brenda, who'd initially invited me to attend an event with her at the mindfulness center. We both attended the silent retreat. I figured if the only benefit I gained was to be in that space I was grateful, since I felt so connected to Saint Francis. I signed up and paid at once. Brenda did also. As I got closer to page 598 (the end), I felt sadness about approaching the end of the book and letting go. My heart was touched deeply by the life of Saint Francis.

So here we are again a year later, and I am a member of the mindfulness center. This is the silent retreat held once a year for both members and nonmembers. Of course, it was life changing and transformational like the other retreats. The following is the description of the retreat topic:

> Franciscan Center, Tampa, Florida, April 19–22, 2018
>
> In the Discourse on the Four Kinds of Nutriments the Buddha describes edible food, sense impressions, volition and consciousness as the nutriments that enable living beings to grow and maintain life. Since we ingest these elements into our bodies and minds, they are responsible for our physical and mental well-being. What we consume, how much we consume and how aware we are of our consumption of the four nutriments are key to our happiness.
>
> Our peace, compassion and well-being, our anger, fear and hatred do not come out of nowhere; they are fed by the choices we make regarding the things we encounter. The habit energies we have developed around edible food, sensory stimuli (including all the ways we absorb information through conversations, reading, use of electronics etc.), volition (the energy that motivates our daily actions), and consciousness (the wholesome or unwholesome seeds that we cultivate and nurture in our mind's consciousness) produce our happiness and our suffering. An understanding of how these processes of nourishment work are fundamental to our life of practice.

In this three-day retreat, we will study and practice the Buddhist teachings on the Four Nutriments. Dharma talks, guided meditations, experiential exercises and group dialogues will help participants nourish the aspiration to cultivate mindfulness in what we take into our bodies and consciousness, clearly see and understand the roots of and suffering caused by the elements we bring into our mind-body, and cultivate "right view" and discipline to support nourishing ourselves in ways that take us in the direction of true mind.

This retreat will be led by senior members. The center leader was present each evening to provide instructions and meditative practices and to interact with retreatants concerning the teachings and practices being offered during the day. As usual, this will be a silent retreat. The silence affords us the opportunity to deepen our meditative experience while absorbing the experiential meaning of the teachings and practices presented.

The retreat was facilitated by three female senior members of the center. I felt so connected to their approach, the content of the retreat, the way they shared experiences about their struggles, and how they utilized the four nutriments below to walk through life consciously:

- Edible foods—the food we consume (wholesome and unwholesome choices)
- Sense impressions—consumption through the five senses
- Volition—intentions and how they impact the flow of energy in our lives (setting our attention on intentions, for which we create desired outcomes, and shifting focus from

unwholesome mind or emotional states as they present
themselves in our experience)

- Consciousness—feeding our mind states with wholesome
  versus unwholesome thoughts. When we water the seeds in
  our consciousness that we want to grow, we will reinforce
  this in our experience and create a support system of
  awareness that consciously supports a choice of what we
  want to manifest outwardly.

On the third and last night, I retreated to my room and sat in
contemplation while icing my back due to the pain and discomfort
I experienced from sitting on the meditation mat for long periods
over three days. I decided to meditate while icing my back. I sat in
silence for a long time. When I came out of my meditative state, I
was compelled to write:

Awareness is expressing through me. I *am*. I am the vehicle
or filter through which life is experienced. I experience awareness
through thoughts, emotions, and my senses. This experience is
not always conscious. It is mostly unconscious, unless awareness
is redirected back at itself, which is mind. When the conscious
behavior/experience is identified and investigated, then this ever-
changing state of mind (consciousness) can be redirected to create
desirable outcomes. In other words, consciousness is becoming
conscious of itself, or mind is becoming aware of itself, or awareness
is becoming aware. It is through me that energy transforms from
unconsciousness to consciousness.

I must choose this though. If it is not a choice, then I will express
my life through mental patterns, mostly living in my mind. This
must tie into free will somehow. However, this only happens through
this vehicle I refer to as my body.

When I live unconsciously, I become stuck in the thought
pattern that I am my body. In this state of consciousness, I believe
that this body—this "me"—is of utmost importance in life. As a
result I am constantly thinking about me—me … me … me …

me … me … me—on and on. I have been going through life only focused on me, either by ruminating in the past or being stuck in the future but never being fully here in my reality.

I have slowed down so much on this retreat that I am able to identify the movement of my mind, and now I understand how my energy moves to any object, person, circumstance, or experience. Usually, I am bringing myself back to the present moment saying, *How did I go down that path anyway?* In this retreat I am learning to be in my body—to be conscious of my beating heart that never stops beating and works tirelessly to keep blood pumping and flowing to all my organs. I am focusing on my breath more, and by setting the intention to be conscious of my breath, I can stay in my body more. If I wander off, following my thoughts or getting swept away by some specific story, I bring myself back to my breathing with awareness.

I can be just a little bit more mindful, and as a result, I see clearly how the mind moves. The universe as we know it becomes a product of the transformation of the collective human consciousness. The more we each live consciously and touch the earth with awareness, the greater the transformation is on the planet. As we become a product of this transformation, evolution speeds up, and the ability to have greater awareness of the nature of mind increases.

And yet I see that the universe is orderly. The grass grows without the involvement of my consciousness. So the collective awareness or universal consciousness as a whole is expressing in unison without my overinflated ego that thinks the universe revolves around me. The entire universe has existed in a state of equanimity. It has thrived despite our disregard for preserving our planet and all life of life itself.

I now have a deeper understanding of the nature of my existence. There is no doubt that everything I experience is a result of causes and conditions previously set in motion. I am on a quest to consciously create my future by consuming foods that are wholesome and nourishing to my body and that cause the least suffering to others including animals. I am doing my best with this last item.

Going forward, I am choosing what I consume through my senses because I understand that what I consume through the senses imprints my mind states, whether consciously or unconsciously. These are the "seeds" that I am watering in my mind. So, I am going to consume things that support peace, joy, happiness, love, harmony, and balance within myself. And by doing so I am choosing to add a little better to the collective consciousness.

I have always been great with working with setting intentions. I am writing my intentions and posting them in my home where I can see and read them every day.

I am committing to consciously looking at my thoughts and emotions and investigating the nature of my thoughts and emotions. I am committing to looking within myself when I am triggered or feel strong emotions so I can investigate and understand the nature of my inner environment. I am going to approach my recurring emotions and thoughts with a sense of curiosity and then challenge the thoughts and emotions with truths. I am also going to follow the motion of energy in my mind before I get wrapped up in a story. I am curious to see how my energy flows to that specific experience that I am apt to get caught up in and maybe play over and over in my mind.

Chapter 9

Contemplating

. . . .

You need to learn how to select
your thoughts just the same way
you select your clothes every day.
This is a power you can cultivate.

—Elizabeth Gilbert

April 29, 2018

I've been contemplating and reflecting on the knowledge gained from the silent retreat. I updated my daily morning affirmation to:

> I wake up grateful for life and the air
> that I breathe knowing that this is a new day and
> there are twenty-four hours ahead of me.
> I intend to live this day
> in mindfulness,
> seeing everything with eyes of compassion.

I've been contemplating the ways I could be more present in all my experiences. How can I break this down into achievable tasks that turn into habits and, ultimately, free myself? I am committing to two things to bring me back to now. They are:

1. Being aware of my breath. This is simply being aware of and feeling my in breath as my body breathes in and observing the natural movement in my midsection as my body breathes out. Sounds easy. And since I have not been in the habit of

constantly having awareness on my breath, this is going to take some time—and patience.

2. Saying "this moment" to bring myself back to this moment when I become aware that I've been lost in thought.

I continue to feel withdrawn after the silent retreat. I'd been feeling resistance around going to the sangha today. I didn't go. I woke up late and decided to paint the walls that were recently patched up from replacing my AC. My home is in disarray from all the work that's been done here. I am feeling the need to reorganize things. I am also feeling the need to focus on my spiritual practice in my own way and on my own time. It seems like what is manifesting in my physical space is what was already shifting energetically for me. I am going to practice. The work being done on my home has left things a state of disarray. I have decided to focus my attention on my two objectives above until this is second nature for me. I decided to commit to mindfulness with every task I approach in my home.

There are so many things going on in my home. There are patches on the wall surrounding all vents in. In addition to the patches from the replacement of AC duct work there is an entire wall that was gutted and replaced. I believe the technical terms used for this replaced wall are "Sheetrock" and "quick-set." There is a new wall in the office! This wall is adjacent to the bathroom. It was gutted and replaced in the last month due to the leaking from the bathroom into the office. This caused mold on the interior of the wall. Instead of treating the mold, I decided to cut out the entire wall completely.

After mold showed up in my blood work in past months, I needed to decide what was causing the mold. The AC was over thirty years old. The ductwork in the home must have been at least thirty years old also. The bathroom is unfinished since the sink is not functional. I can live with this for now. The bathroom cabinet was built by Marie's dad, Philippe. Once the quartz is cut in proportion to the sink, Philippe will install the cabinet and have a plumber connect the sink. The process for cutting the quartz countertop and attaching it to the cabinet will take about three to four weeks. We expect to have this done by mid to late May. The flooring and toilet were also replaced, and once complete, the entire bathroom will feel new—except for the old tub. This work took an entire month. Finally, I can start painting and making this home feel like home again. I am excited to paint and deepen my spiritual practice.

I picked up supplies at Home Depot. I felt overwhelmed when I got back to the house. So much stuff—where do I start? First things first! I needed to turn on some music to get a little inspiration. I have been hooked on the *Light is the New Black* playlist, and it is perfect for this activity.

Once the music was going, I needed to decide which room to start on. The walls around all AC vents had been patched. In the kitchen that part of the ceiling is blue. Okay! I purchased the paint! The vent in my bedroom is not on the ceiling, so I must use the paint that was used on bedroom walls. When the old container of paint was opened today at Home Depot, the clerk advised that I could still use the paint purchased some eight years ago—I believe. She was not able to determine the exact color, since the barcode was faded. In the office, I would prime the new wall and then pick out a blue I liked from the swatch of colors I'd brought home. Then there was white ceiling that was patched up. I observed as my mind analyzed how to tackle the job:

Start with priming and prime all of the patches in all the rooms.

Well that just supports your undiagnosed ADD.

Paint completely in one room at a time.

Then I'll have to have a paint liner filled with primer and the other colors also.

Well you could just start with the primer and work on the color for one room.

Hmmmm.

How about the bedroom? Let's get the bedroom completely painted and everything else primed.

So that's what I did. I laid drop cloths down everywhere. I taped the areas that were not being painted. I put down a garbage bag on the chair in my room with the hand brush I was about to use, as well as the roller. I realized I only had one roller. So I would need to complete priming and then replace the roller to paint the gray walls in the bedroom. As I poured the primer and primed the bedroom first, I paid attention to the way the paint looked as it was being poured. I realized that I was feeling this strong need to retreat because I had these wonderful tools to practice mindfulness, and it was only theoretical if I didn't practice.

In that moment, I decided that I was going to spend the rest of my year reinforcing my habit energy with being present in this moment. I also decided that I was going to take a hiatus from the local Mindfulness Center. I had all the tools I needed for mindfulness, and I wasn't interested in learning any theoretical information right now. My sole purpose would be to slow down enough so that I was always aware of my breathing. Even if I as wandering off in my mind, I wanted to be focused on the breath, so that I could be grounded in this moment.

As I started painting, I quickly got lost in the up and down and even side brushstrokes. It occurred to me that the most effective way to be my own mindfulness trainer in the coming months was to map out some projects and be fully submerged in them as I did them. I felt excitement due to the thought prior to that, being, *Now I see how disorganized this house is and how stuff is just moved from room to room to make space for work being done. It's time to tidy things up.*

So, I completed the bedroom and primed the kitchen and the new wall in the office. I was going to become a hermit in the coming months. As I took a break and decided to hand-feed Petey, I noticed the movement of his eyes when he was eating. He looked down at the food; looked at my fingers (which he is currently terrified of, and hand-feeding is a way of building trust); and then looked up at my eyes. I kept my eyes focused on his eyes, and every time he looked up, we made eye contact for that quick second before he looked back down again.

I am so grateful for these moments. I am grateful to be able to capture a moment looking into his beautiful eyes. I believe these moments are eternal moments. They make my heart happy and joyful. Today, whenever I looked over at Petey while painting, he was always looking at me. Every time I looked over while painting the bedroom, he was looking right at me—all fluffed up and happy.

Today I noticed while I was taking a shower that he was doing his distress call. I called back at him to let him know I was here even though he couldn't see me. And when I emerged from the bathroom, his eyes were right on me. He teaches me a lot about being present.

It's the end of the day, and I am alone. It's a full moon tonight. I'm choosing to spend all my alone moments being happy in my own company. There are really fewer moments alone in our lives than there are moments with others—friends, family, acquaintances, strangers, or even pets. The few rare alone moments are a gift for me to be fully present in my experience and know what it is like to be with me without thinking about anything else.

April 30, 2018

I am officially in hermit mode, and what this means is that I am on a mission to increase mindfulness and live in my current reality in front of me. I will keep all commitments that are on the calendar so I can learn to be fully mindful while submerged in interaction with others. Mind is constantly funneling unconscious thoughts, and my awareness deepens. Today I had a little more success focusing on my breath than I did yesterday. There is progress. I woke up and stated my intentions and then began my day.

Last night, I wrote out my weekly goals. There is nothing better than establishing structure around desired goals, so there are no excuses or scattered energy. I am more likely to be present if I know what I'm supposed to do in the morning, afternoon, and evening. I am 100 percent invested in achieving this in the next three months. There is little room for deviation, unless of course, I choose to be defiant—aka self-Sabotage. So, here was my outline for today:

1. Catch up on work emails (it's never ending, and I never really catch up, but I stay consistently behind).
2. Pick up new station for Petey. The mirror in Petey's station where he is fed broke, and he is skeptical of going to the makeshift station. He is being trained since he is resistant to go into the cage when I am leaving the house, and the trainer suggested placing a station on the door. This station will be the only place where he receives his favorite treats. It's working, and he loves just hanging out there. Besides, it's easy to close the door and not have to handle him, which has resulted in him being terrified of my hands. I have had to chase him around and pick him up to put him in the cage. I don't like doing it either, and if he is able to have the door closed while he is on the station, he interprets going into the cage as being part of his decision. Getting a new station is top priority! I accomplished it during lunch. I picked up two!
3. Finish documentation for project at work.
4. Write for fifteen minutes.
5. Exercise.
6. Read myManifesto.
7. Read fifteen minutes of *You're a Badass* by Jen Sincero.

While working I realize that I feel overwhelmed when there are a few tasks to be accomplished. I often water the seeds of overwhelm in my workday. With this awareness, I am choosing to slow down, breathe, and work with what is in front of me and only that one task. And all work gets done anyway. My chance of being more productive increases because I am calm and at ease, instead of being freaking frantic all the time. The simple choice to breathe in and breathe our while focusing on the specific task at hand helps. Then

I can breathe in and breathe out while focusing on the next task. The key is keeping the consciousness of my breath in my peripheral vision (so to speak).

Amazing, wonderful things are happening now that I've set the intention to exist in the present moment being mindful and accepting the reality of life in front of me as my primary state of being. At the end of the day, I completed all the tasks I needed to complete today.

Later in the day as I was driving back from the pet store, I was aware of my mind going over some thoughts. There was, *I'm happy, becoming more mindful, and facing my reality.* Some negative thoughts crept in:

> First thought. *You don't really have to this mindfulness stuff because no one is going to know.*
>
> Next thought. *No. Back off because I made a commitment, and you know as well as I do that, when I have my eye on the target, I'm unstoppable. Push through.*
>
> Next thought. *Well who do you have to prove anything to?*
>
> Next thought. *It's not about proving anything. It's about living my life in the space where there is no time because mind does not exist in front of me. So why live there? Doesn't it make more sense to be with what I am experiencing through my senses?*
>
> Next thought. *Awareness being aware of itself is making a claim for the unconscious state of my being.*
>
> Next thought. *I know that what I experienced for those five minutes was real, so there is no way I am not doing this.*

One of the keys to being successful at this is to be very aware of what I am consuming through my senses throughout the day. I heard the birds chirping outside today. As I walked out, a mockingbird was making the most beautiful sounds and looking right at me. I stood there for a while and as I stared at the bird. I felt the warmth of the afternoon sun on my face. Listening to birds is symbolic of watering the positive seeds within my consciousness.

I've decided the TV will only be turned on twice a week, maybe on Friday and Saturday. Honestly, I probably turned the TV on five times in the last couple months, and it's not on purpose. I've been reading a lot and simply enjoying silence in the home. It's nice.

I have listened to affirmations by *Dream Manifesto* for the last month while hanging out with Petey in the evening. I listened to them today on my walk. I also listen to a guided meditation on Insight Timer by Sarah Blondin, "Loving and Listening to Yourself" at the end of my workday. This meditation recenters me. I read my manifesto and will meditate and go to bed. Feeding my mind with the seeds of positivity nurtures a positive state of mind in me and is just as important as ensuring that I eat at least 70 percent vegetables in my daily diet.

I am remembering to always have attention on my body breathing in and breathing out, no matter what I am doing or thinking:

Breathing in

Breathing out

In this moment

Chapter 10

Persisting

. . . .

Vulnerability is not weakness.
Vulnerability is our most accurate
measurement of courage.
—Dr. Brené Brown, Ted talk

May 1, 2018

Persistence prevails when all else fails! I was mostly in an unconscious state today, with moments of bringing myself back to my breath and wondering how I could be doing so great yesterday and today it seems like "this moment" is so far away. I have a feeling this chapter is going to be really long. There is no other way to start a new way of living after doing things one way for forty-four years. I cannot expect things to be different overnight. Of course, my mind enjoys being in the unconscious state of the sea of thoughts that randomly flow in and out. My tendency is to attach to my emotional state that is typically my habit energy. I also know that I cannot think through this if I expect to get to the next step in the process. So the basic—very, very basic—action I must practice is just being aware of two things:

Breathing in

Breathing out

And when I become aware that I am caught up in mind, I bring myself to say, "This moment," and come back to looking at and naming the things in front of me.

I am certain that, with persistence, I will develop the habit of always being aware of the movement of my chest area when I breathe in and out, and this will be the new focal point of my attention.

It's all about attention, and I really believe that energy flows where attention goes. Keeping my attention on my chest also keeps me aware of my beating heart, which supports my existence tirelessly every moment of every day throughout my life. This is my goal in every moment. Maybe tomorrow will be a better day.

May 2, 2018

There is a small improvement in the actual awareness of my breathing in and breathing out. Yeah, this is a job for a person who has withstood many ups and downs in life and knows that the only way out is consistency. So here I am—committed! Nothing is going to make me stop at this point because part of me wants to see if this mindfulness stuff is pure bullstuff and to test whether it makes no difference whether I live the in the reality in front of me or whether I choose to live in my mind. Since I had the experience of pure bliss for maybe five minutes that day while lying on the couch with Petey, I am hungry for more. So I will continue. The degree to which I can accept and allow what is in front of me to be my perception of reality is the degree to which I will succeed. It is also the degree of acceptance in my being of the truth about what is reality. Ultimately the truth is not the delusive stories in my mind. It is the here and now.

This quote by Thich Nhat Hanh—which I read last night after I was done writing—was in the *Everyday Mindfulness* book dated May 1: "Mindfulness helps you go home to the present. And every time you go there and recognize a condition of happiness that you have, happiness comes."

This reminds me to come back to being fully present. When I am aware of my breath as my constant during my experience, I can acknowledge my happiness in those moments. By doing so, I am inviting more happiness. As I open to allowing and accepting life exactly as it is in front of me, I can perceive true moments of joy with ease. My awareness and understanding of happiness deepen. I am no longer waiting for something to make me happy. I am being happy with life in front of me. I am allowing each moment to open my heart to the beauty in front of me. A shift is occurring from my mental construct of happiness to my experience of happiness. In order to water the seeds of positivity in my consciousness or simply shift my consciousness to a state of greater well-being, I only need to recognize and acknowledge the things that create my joy when I am in "this moment."

This is another simple aspect of shifting my consciousness. For example, today at lunch with a coworker, I was able to be conscious of my breathing as the foundation of my being, and then we reflected on something that was funny. I reinforced joy as a positive seed of being in the present moment. If I do this often enough, it will become the new pattern in my being. I still think this chapter is going to be very long, and I am committed to keeping it authentic. Who knows? Maybe I will really evolve as a person who exists in the present moment.

May 3, 2018

Slight progress today—I am more aware of my breathing in and breathing out. I am in my body more than I am living in my mind. I noticed at the retreat that, when I am in my body, everything slows down more. The longer I stay in my body, time seems even slower and slower, and everything about me resonates with the life around me. It's like I am vibrating with the trees and the wildlife around me. I also noticed that there is a lightness slightly off center from my left eyebrow—a feeling of there being an opening in that space. Today I felt this space over my left brow in the afternoon and evening.

Breathing in

Breathing out

In this moment

May 4, 2018

This is so hard.

May 5, 2018

I just experienced several minutes of no thought while lying on the couch with Petey. This happened between 7:00 and 7:49 p.m. Petey was sitting on my big toe, and at one point, I felt the pulse in my toe throbbing under his toes, and it felt like his toes were part of my body. Thought crept in, and I lay and followed my breathing. It sounded deep and heavy. I felt heat from the base of my midsection rising to the top of my head. I felt my heart beating. There is a sound to silence, like a constant humming, and if I really listen to it and focus on it while looking into Petey's eyes and while feeling my heartbeat and being aware of my breathing, then there is no room for thoughts. There is that lightness slightly off center closer to my left eyebrow. I felt it the whole time while on the couch, and there were many moments when Petey became a blur in front of me.

Just earlier today, I was sitting at the salon and observing the thoughts that were coming up as I breathed in and out. I have been observing the nature of my thoughts. And what do you know? It's the same stuff over and over. I can safely say that I am now aware of what I am thinking of all the time.

I am not ruminating about the past. Thank goodness! No, instead I am fantasizing about the future. What is the guy I will meet going to look like? And how much he is going to love and adore me?

I painted two and a half walls with primer after work yesterday. I realized that the roller missed the crevices in the textured wall, and there where big gaps of the color beige in between patches of white. I got the paint brush out and hand painted the entire wall again. And while I was watching the brush go up and down, I noticed I had so many thoughts like:

Mindfulness equals patience.

Because watching this brush go up and down and sideways isn't hard enough, I have to actually jab it into the uneven textured parts, so I actually cover up the beige.

Mindfulness equals patience.

Because not only am I going to have to prime this one wall that was replaced, I am going to have to prime the entire room, or the blue will look different on the walls that have beige on them.

So, no half-assedness.

And now that Philippe made me get glossy white for the baseboards, I will have to paint that with the right color. Now that I have that knowledge I have to do it right, since the perfectionist in me will never let me live it down otherwise.

And while I'm getting the baseboards right, I'm going to have to paint the patched-up, primed ceiling with the eggshell white paint that Peaches at Home Depot picked out for the ceiling. Oh, and I still have to paint the entire room in blue, with two coats.

Did I say that all this mindfulness and being present is really just about learning patience?

Because when I escape to the fantasy of what my future love might be like, I just come back to:

Mindfulness equals patience—because he is not here now. So again, patience.

At least I am aware of my breathing most of the times, and at least my thoughts were mostly about what is in front of me.

I read this today while sitting patiently at the salon as the student covered up my grays and highlighted my hair while dabbing color all over my face, and I smiled patiently:

There's a statistic that says only 5 percent of people who sign up for something, like a course or a seminar, actually do anything with it. And this includes very, very, very high-priced somethings, not just the money-management class at the community college down the road. This is because lots of people wish for change, really, really want it, are willing to invest the time and money into it, but are ultimately not willing to get uncomfortable enough to actually make anything happen. Which means they don't want it as badly as they say they do. "I tried" is the poor man's "I kicked butt." (Jen Sincero, *You Are a Badass*)

How did she know? It was exactly the pep talk I needed. I'm doing it, damn it! So, I am going to eat dinner mindfully and go back to painting the one and a half walls that need to be primed. By the way, it's Saturday at 8:41 p.m. It's not like I am going to choose to be mindless on Saturdays, so I might as well include Saturdays.

It's 11:50 p.m. There is a sense of accomplishment when one transitions from brushstrokes in every direction only to see that the entire room is painted. I'm happy that I primed the entire room. I only noticed tonight that the paint container has words like "stain blocker" on it—a very important feature, of course.

I am intending to be operating from my *present* experience of reality 70 percent of the time by my birthday in July. I have about two and a half months to do this. I'm crazy to put this in writing. I absolutely, positively want this more than I want anything else in my life, and I am taking the steps and doing the work. Holy stuff!

May 7, 2018

This moment is my reality. Can I be fully attentive with mundane tasks and be calm and at ease doing them? After all, they're all mundane tasks. I'm noticing that I am forever reaching for what's next. I question, Am I willing to change? Am I willing to give myself a chance to be with what I am doing and to be here now continuously? Am I willing to give myself an opportunity to do everything with my full attention being on the task at hand? Can I experience a sense of ease with what is in front of me right now? Am I curious enough about what it might be like to accept this moment exactly as it presents?

Can I choose to be present with myself right now and be in my body, at ease with my reality, and not choose to go somewhere else in my mind? This last question is my epiphany.

In the words of Jen Sincero, in *You Are a Badass*, "An epiphany is a visceral understanding of something you already know."

May 9, 2018

I felt in the dumps as I went to bed last night. I was overcome with fear that this process is crap, and I am wasting time trying to do this because it's basically just about accepting where I'm at now and realizing that everything is always changing. So how do others exist in the present moment? Like Eckhart Tolle?

I know, in the love of my being, I can practice my way into being completely mindful in the present moment and be able to use thought instead of thought using me. I am continuing with my personal experiment. This will be conducted in my lab—aka, home—and all other places I am. And I am sure this is right for me because I am more eager about doing it than about anything else in my life.

Since being superfocused has worked for me up to this point in my life, I will use this focus in my process. Mindfulness becomes the strongest muscle in my being. This is exactly why I am working out—so I can strengthen the mindfulness muscle. The only path I am following is my own.

May 10, 2018

I am painting the ceiling now. It looks great. The blue on the walls is called "bluebird," and I love it. I am enjoying using the roller on the ceiling and feeling light, joyous, and happy.

At 11:51 p.m., I am done painting. Pepper was here this evening. Earlier, Petey kept looking over at her cage. He was on his food bowl on my stomach and then on my big toe, always looking over at her cage. I heard a shuffling over by the picture frame in front of the fireplace. I looked over there for a while and nothing was there. *She is here*, I thought.

I said, "Pepper are you here?"

Petey, for once, was not looking at me. He looked over at her cage so intently the whole time, and nothing could distract him.

May 14, 2018

I cleaned and rearranged the entire house. I moved the cabinet that was blocking the front door back into the office. I'm still bringing myself back to my breath and having more and more moments of being fully focused and present with whatever I am doing. The office was completed this weekend, and I'm going to start on the hallway. I'm going to prime the walls now.

May 15, 2018

Shawn and I are heading to Sarasota to shop and have some lunch. I am going to receive a massage before we start our trip. Today would have been my sixth wedding anniversary with my ex-husband—if we were still married.

Thoughts creep in that marriage is mostly a failed institution. Statistics show that 50 percent of marriages end in divorce; of my marriages, 100 percent have ended in divorce. I rest my case.

In order to truly honor my vow to the present moment I am going to let the future take care of itself.

May 18, 2018

The final stages of completing the work in my bathroom are nearing. My bathroom sink was installed tonight. After building and installing the sink, Philippe put me in touch with a plumber he works with, James. James and Danny were here today and installed the bathroom sink. It is so nice to have a functioning bathroom that looks so beautiful. The bathroom is complete. In addition to installing my sink, James adjusted the temperature on the hot water heater so that I can have hot baths. This is nice, since I usually boil water on the stove to add to my bath. I am grateful.

May 22, 2018

I have spent the past three days mindlessly enjoying my home. There've been moments of mindfulness with my work on the home and when editing the second book I'm writing. Today I'm catching myself shallow breathing and really can't seem to stop myself from going off with random thoughts. Mindfulness is not the path of least resistance. Coming back to my breathing in "this moment."

At 2:37 p.m., Brenda texted that she realized her mind was all over the place while getting a massage last night. I assured her that I do it also. It is so hard to enjoy my massage when I am not in my body. When I am almost at the end of the massage, I relax. If only I would do that from the beginning, I could feel more relaxed and be in my body for the entire massage.

I know the pain and tension in my muscles, especially my shoulders and neck, have been speaking to me. This pain is trying to get my attention. This pain is urging me to get out of my head and be in my body. Feel my feet walking the earth. Feel what my heartbeat feels like in the middle of my chest. Breathe in and out and know that I am alive, and this is a gift.

Another quote from Jen Sincero's *You Are a Badass:*

> Once something moves from our brains to our bones, that's when we can use it to change our lives.
>
> The million-dollar question is, will we?
>
> Oh, the years people spend talking the talk, rolling out the shoulds, woulds and coulds, attending classes, trolling the seminar circuit, and burying themselves in all sorts of shelf-helper before they finally, if ever, DO anything with it all.

Chapter 11

Jolting

· ·

May the new lines on our maps bring
good things to the world.
—from the movie *Here* with Ben Foster and Lubna Azabal

July 6, 2018

What I am about to share is not happening here in the moment. As you read, you will understand why I could not write about it before now. I have a nervous feeling in my gut right now, and this is taking a lot of courage. On June 24, 2018, it was a hot sunny day. My friend James wanted to go to the beach and invited me to join him. He wanted to drive down to Siesta Key and was eager to snorkel. I had no plans that day and decided to be in the moment. In my beach bag, I packed some sunscreen, a couple beach towels, and *Love Warrior* (a memoir) by Glennon Doyle.

It was around 9:30 a.m. when we took off. We drove down to Siesta Key in James's car. We stopped for coffee and gas at the Wawa, and James got a burrito. As I walked up to the counter, the clerk smiled, proclaiming, "You are both going to have a fun day at the beach."

Realizing that James had already shared our plans, I smiled and turned my head slightly left. And as our eyes met, James shot a smile at me. I sensed how excited he felt to share this adventure with me. He was already outside as I approached the door, and he walked back in and held the consecutive doors open for me.

Back in his car, James ate his burrito. He shared that it contained egg whites, spinach, chicken, salsa, and jalapenos. It was an odd combination of ingredients, I thought. Knowing that we both shared a love for hot peppers, he commented that the jalapenos had a kick, yanked one out from the top of the burrito, reached over, and fed it to me. The pepper was, indeed, hotter than jalapenos I have tasted in store-bought burritos. I reluctantly took a bite of the burrito, and to my surprise it was delicious—mouthwateringly delicious. I mentioned that I would be remembering to stop at Wawa for a breakfast burrito soon.

On the drive, we chatted, listened to music, and sang along. James shared his excitement to drive his Infiniti, since the engine had been rebuilt in the past week and the car had been returned a couple days prior. I don't have an interest in cars or their ability to perform. However, I was most interested in being fully present with what was being shared, and I observed that James was being fully present with me also. He sped up on the highway to demonstrate the ease at which his car accelerates. There was a soft hum to the engine. The traffic was light on the highway. I recall James accelerating up to 130 miles per hour briefly and then decelerating. Fearless, I laughed with excitement.

We talked and shared so much and somehow missed the exit for Siesta Key. Half an hour later, we realized we were heading to Venice and turned around. James giggled, radiating a roaring belly laugh in my direction. He was laughing hysterically about not paying attention as we drifted off way past our exit. His laughter was very distinct. His presence, gentle and kind. I gravitated toward this laughter on the day I'd first met him when he'd installed my bathroom sink. His distinctive giggle was very infectious. I mentioned I could have been helpful with directions. In truth, I much preferred being present with whatever we were sharing in the moment. Hail praises to the GPS, we arrived around 11:30ish.

We got out of the car, and James realized that his swim trunks were not in the trunk of the car. I mentioned that we could go buy a pair, since there were tons of beach shops around. But he was not up for doing that and decided he could swim in the jersey shorts he was wearing. He latched his keys onto the drawstring of his shorts.

I motioned to the beach bag now hanging from my shoulder and mentioned I could carry them in my beach bag so he wouldn't have to deal with the weight of the keys attached to his waist. He didn't go for that option.

James reached into his trunk and pulled out another hook. He then hooked it onto the first hook that was on his shorts and showed me that there was no way the keys could fall off while snorkeling because it was hooked onto two clasps and knotted onto the drawstring of his pants.

We locked up, and on the way in, I hit the restroom while James walked around under the pavilion. We talked about getting lunch at the pavilion later. As we were walking onto the beach, James pointed to the seagulls and mentioned that they looked old. I agreed. We stopped and observed the birds for a while. I felt at peace. I was happy that James noticed the birds. We talked about how nice it is to see birds wild and free.

Within ten minutes of walking on the beach, we were drenched in sweat. We started to walk in the water. It helped to cool us off. We laughed as the waves crashed into the shoreline and almost knocked me down a couple of times. We walked further into the water, feeling the coolness of the water splashing on our legs.

James pointed off in the distance to the area where he wanted to snorkel—Point of Rocks. He mentioned he could swim out there in fifteen minutes. I suggested he do that, and I could walk out and meet him out there.

He looked at me and replied, "That's not very considerate."

We were heading south on the beach and walked down the beach quite a distance, maybe a mile or more from where we were parked.

While walking, we passed a couple, and the man was saying, "You can walk if you want to, but I'm not walking."

We laughed hysterically, and I looked over at James and said, "That makes you a true gentleman," because he didn't want me to walk the beach alone.

Shortly after, James mentioned that we could probably set up on the beach. We swam for a while and talked, and then James took off swimming south to his snorkel spot. I watched him swim away. I noticed how, every time I turned away for a few minutes and looked back, he still had his eyes peeled on me, even though he was swimming in the opposite direction. I stayed in the water for a long time enjoying the sun and the coolness of the water against my skin. The waves were crashing in. I moved closer to the beach and lay on the sand, half-submerged in the water.

As I looked back and around to locate James in the water, I noticed that there were more people in the water. I lost track of where he was. I relaxed into the moment, feeling the waves gently caving into the sand and washing over my body. It was a lovely day. The seagulls were squawking. I observed them landing on the sand and walking briskly and busily going about their business.

After a while, I got out of the water and headed over to my spot on the beach. I lay on my beach towel and read for a while and then went back into the water to cool off. A couple hours passed by.

I noticed some dark clouds south of where I was lying, in the direction where James was swimming. The sun was out and blazing hot. I continued to go in and out of the water to cool off. My book was getting really good. I was getting lost in the story when the raindrops started pattering onto the pages. I had no idea what time it was, since we'd left our phones in the trunk of James's car.

The raindrops started coming down a little harder and the pages of my book were becoming damp. Soon after, I looked up, and there was no one in the water. The raindrops were constant now. James was nowhere in sight. I decided to put everything back in my beach bag. I covered the bag with one of the beach towels. I left the bag on the beach shawl and started walking south on the beach. I figured James would be walking back and decided to walk in the direction he would be approaching from.

I walked for about ten minutes, and then I spotted him. He had a huge smile on his face. I asked, "Did you have fun?"

He smiled and replied, "The water was clear and beautiful."

He leaned forward, and our lips met. He shared that he had a great time and mentioned he ran into a pool of dead yucky things, and other than that, it was a great time. The sky was becoming gray, and the raindrops were constant now.

As I am writing now, "I Love the Rain Most (when it stops)" by Joe Purdy just started playing on Spotify.

The rain continued to fall at a steady pace. The beach was sparse, and although there was rain, we had no reason to be scared since it wasn't thundering. We walked back briskly on the beach toward the south side public parking lot of Siesta Key where we were parked. We picked up my bag, and James suggested I cover it with the beach towel to keep the contents as dry as possible.

We jumped over dirty water coming down in streams from the buildings adjacent to the beach. The raindrops were becoming more frequent and the atmosphere gloomy. James was tired and mentioned that he wanted me to drive back.

At one point, I remember him looking over into my eyes and saying, "This is so great. I love the rain."

I smiled and exclaimed, "I love the rain too."

The rain started to pour down, and we picked up the pace, walking faster. We were hustling to get off the beach. We walked faster and faster. Out of nowhere came a torrential downpour within a few minutes. We were both drenched.

James was now about a half step ahead of me walking on my right side. Suddenly, I felt a shock. From the corner of my right eye, I saw a flash of light, a thin spark next to the right side of my head. It appeared about half a foot away from my body, slightly above my head. I realized it was lightning. It looked like the lightning I'd seen in the sky, except this glimpse was barely noticeable, and it was probably the length of my hand. That was all I could see in the split second before I felt the impact to my body.

Immediately, I started to feel a buzzing, tingling sensation in my brain and was confused. There was no time for thinking. I was taken by surprise. The electrical sensation became stronger. It started pulsing in my brain, and I slowed my pace in reaction. James was now in front of me. Unable to process what was happening, I lost control of the beach bag, and its contents fell to the sand. The pulsation became more of a surge, and I felt it spread down my neck, around my shoulders, and then in my chest. The impulse around my heart was much stronger than it felt in my brain.

It occurred to me that I could be dying. It was constricting, and I crisscrossed my arms over my chest to resist the intensity of the impulse. It felt overwhelming. I felt like I'd been shocked by an electrical socket, except the intensity was maybe ten thousand times more. I can't begin to explain how intense it was.

I turned slightly right as I felt myself go wobbly and tried to keep myself from falling. The pulsating feeling intensified as it flowed into my legs. I felt the electricity moving through my body, and there was a strong tingling electrical sensation in my lower legs from my knees down to my feet. I looked down at my feet, and I could barely feel my feet connecting to my Teva flip-flops.

Like a blow—*voom!*—I was propelled backward. The intensity was just as strong as or stronger than the intensity of the impulse I'd felt in my chest. Before I could blink, I found myself on the ground. I was blown back maybe three feet. I fell on the sand on my bottom with my forearms slightly behind my body. My forearms landed on the sand as my body tilted back slightly. Time stopped.

I reoriented myself and searched for James. I couldn't feel my body. I looked up and saw a spark to the right of James's head. This spark was bigger and longer than the one I had just seen. The angle of my vision seemed unusual. I was looking at him from an angle not familiar. It seemed like I was stretched out and forward in front and slightly above my body. I could not feel my body.

I had no sensation, and yet I needed to move forward because I felt like I was dying, and I couldn't allow this to happen to him. I was grasping and reaching, but my body was not responding. Still on my bottom with my elbows planted in the sand, I started yelling his name over and over, and the strangest thing happened. I couldn't hear myself. I couldn't feel my body. And I was screaming, "James," over and over, and I could not hear my own voice. I tried to move, but I couldn't move.

I saw a spark appearing at the level of his waist. He was standing in place, frozen. Even though there was a downpour, and we were caught in a thunderstorm, it seemed totally silent, and everything stopped. I continued to scream, "James."

The stillness soaked in, and I stopped. Everything stopped. I watched helplessly as I saw James's head drop. I tried with everything I had to move. My body was not cooperating. I kept trying to move and continued calling out his name. Nothing happened. I saw James fall face forward onto the sand. He fell straight over and lay facedown on the sand.

Still, I couldn't move, and I needed to save him from this horrible freak accident that was occurring. I fought with everything I had in me to roll myself over onto my right—*everything*! It was not working. I tried again and was able to push onto my hands but still could not completely feel my body. I was panicking and searching for strength.

I dragged myself onto my knees and crawled over to his side. I reached over and touched his neck. I heard the thundering above. I knew the storm was still happening, and we needed to get under cover. I said his name over and over, and he was not responding. I noticed the flippers under his left arm were smoking. I yanked them out from under his arm and threw them with the goggles. I tried to move him. I couldn't. I shook him a bit and panicked. I started calling for help. I searched for my legs and pushed with all my strength.

I stood up and looked around. There were two guys to the left on the beach, a close distance away. I started waving at them, calling. Scared. Crying.

One of the guys ran over. I told him James had been struck by lightning, and he wasn't responding. We needed to roll him over to do CPR. We tried to roll him over, and we didn't have the strength.

The kind stranger said he was going to call 9-1-1. I waited for a few minutes. The rain continued to pour, and the thunder was rolling above. It seemed like an eternity since the guy had left, so I decided to go get others to help with CPR. I ran into the direction the stranger was headed in. As I approached the condominium building to the right off the beach, I begged the strangers to come help and asked if anyone knew CPR.

Two kind ladies came out to assist. They took turns. We moved a tent that was abandoned over him to cover his body. They administered CPR without stopping. Then one of the ladies made us move the tent away. She said she wasn't getting a pulse.

I felt like the ambulance was taking forever and ran back to the building to call 9-1-1 again. The kind lady who was initially helping administer CPR was staying at the condo. When I approached the building, she came up to me and gave me a hug and took me to the security office, where I called 9-1-1. The dispatcher informed me that they'd received the first call, and emergency services were on their way. I headed back out to the beach.

When I arrived on the beach, James was in the back of the lifeguard's truck. Passersby were assisting the lifeguards doing chest compressions on him in the back of the truck. There were three to four men in the back of the lifeguard's truck. The lifeguard signaled at me to get into the truck because we were leaving.

I quickly grabbed our things within reach that were scattered on the beach and left the rest behind. I mentioned to the lifeguard that I believed his keys were on the beach, and he assured me he would locate them later. We were driven off the beach while the four men in the bed of the truck performed chest compressions on James. I remember looking back there the whole time. When I wasn't, I looked ahead as the truck drove off slowly, thinking it was taking way too long to get off the beach. I realized how far south we were on the beach as the lifeguard drove off the beach with the sirens on. I couldn't believe we'd walked that far south. I kept looking back in the trailer of the truck where the men worked on James while the rain poured down. My dress was drenched. I was cold, and I felt scared.

The ambulance was parked in front of James's car. I mentioned to the lifeguard that that was his car. He was transferred to the ambulance, and they asked me to sit up front. I kept my gaze focused on the back of the ambulance. They put an IV in his arm. Although I didn't have a clear view of what they were doing, I could see the EMTs were working on him the whole time.

The hospital was only fifteen minutes away, and it felt like it took two hours to get there. I was so scared. I was praying Psalm 23. And I don't recall the last time I'd prayed. I was so afraid, I started begging the universe for James to be okay.

We arrived at the ER, and as they were taking the gurney out of the ambulance, I heard one of the paramedics say, "He's gone."

I lost it. I felt time stop, and my entire universe caved in. It didn't register fully.

Everything after that moment seemed so surreal. They took me into a room, and within five minutes, there was a doctor in front of me saying James was not alive—except he used different words like maybe "deceased."

I looked at him thinking, *Why does he state this so matter-of-factly? Nonchalant.*

I didn't believe it. The hospital employees all spoke to me so casually—impersonal. I was frozen in disbelief and remember thinking, *This is not true. This is not reality. I am having a dream. I am going to wake up soon. Wake up! Wake up! Wake up!*

Except I did not wake up. Everything after that moment was unbelievable, and yet I had to be with it fully. There was no escape because it was reality. This was actually happening!

A social worker asked if I had contacts for family. I had nothing. I did not have my phone or his. Nor did I know any of his family or friends. I'd met James six weeks earlier through my friend Marie's dad when he worked on installing my bathroom sink in my home.

He installed the sink on the evening of May18. I'd also met his best friend and roommate who was with him that night, Danny.

The medical team brought me into the room where James was lying on the bed. I held his hand. It was warm. I thought I saw him move. I saw his eyes twitch when I was alone with him in the room. I mentioned to the social worker that she should call Marie and ask her to have her dad call their employer and get James's emergency contact info. The social worker came back and said that it was a wrong number. I asked her to google the name of Marie's business, and she did.

In the meantime, the police talked with me. I talked to the sheriff first. He asked me details I did not know about names of James's family members. I didn't know much and told him that the info they needed was in the car, and the lifeguard was going to retrieve the keys that we'd left behind on the beach. The sheriff left and said he would be back.

Once everyone left, I was alone with James. I kept saying, "James come back, come back," over and over again and again. I sobbed. I held his hand and touched his fingers, feeling the warmth. I didn't believe he wasn't alive. I looked at his fingers and memorized the shape of his fingers and hands. I held his hand and interlaced it with mine. I knew he was still alive. Maybe they didn't realize it. I looked at the details of his fingers and his nails. It has been mentally imprinted in my mind.

I said to James, "Your hand is warm. I know you are going to wake up."

I looked at his face and swore he twitched. I reached over his body, and looking at his face, I waited for him to open his eyes. He didn't. I waited a few seconds.

I moved over and bent over him, lifted his right eyelid and looked into his eyes, and said, "Are you there?"

There was no answer.

I sobbed uncontrollably.

The hospital staff was in and out of the room. Everyone worked together to gather information in order to reach his family. They asked me a few times if I wanted to be checked out, and I said no. There was no space in my heart to worry about me.

Marie returned the call, and the social worker brought the phone into the room. I told Marie that I was at the beach with James and there had been an accident. Marie had no idea who James was. She asked me if I was okay. I shared that I was okay, "But he is not okay." I explained that James worked with her dad, and we needed to get in touch with his family.

She didn't seem to understand what I was saying. I was so out of sorts that I did not explain to Marie that our phones were in the car, and she did not understand why I needed to have her dad get the emergency contacts from their employer. I told her I needed her to come to the hospital, *now*. She said she was on her way.

She later explained that she could not understand me on the phone because I was so frantic, and she only understood that there was an accident and did not know we had been struck by lightning. She was in bed sick, when the social worker had called and explained that there was a terrible accident and her friend Karen was in the hospital and needed her to come. Marie loves me so much that, even though she was very ill, she dropped everything and drove two hours to the hospital in the midst of a thunderstorm.

The hospital staff moved me back into the waiting area. The chaplain came in, and there were two detectives there also. They took a recorded statement of the events as I'd witnessed them. I mentioned to them that our IDs were in James's car, and the lifeguard and sheriff were going to locate the keys and get in touch with me later. I remember telling the detective I didn't understand why this was happening. I wished it was me instead, and he looked right at me and said, "It's not your time."

The chaplain sitting in the chair to the right of me verbally agreed.

This was not comforting. I did not want to be comforted anyway. I wanted to erase the whole accident. I wanted us to walk off the beach and head home safely—both of us!

The chaplain walked me to the bathroom, where the ER was located. As I was heading back to the room, I saw Marie. I recall her arms wrapping around me and holding me. I lost it in that moment. I was happy to see her. We got back to the room, and we both sat down next to James. I explained who James was, and she informed me that her dad had already been in touch with Danny.

We sat there in disbelief. I said, "I don't know why this is happening."

Marie shared that she didn't know either, but she mentioned that she'd realized on the drive down that it was a "wake-up call" for her, because she'd wondered if she could live without me being here. She looked at James and said, "I could've been picking you up like that."

Silently, in that moment, I wished it was me and not him. We sat there and looked at James. I continued to cry and repeat, "James, come back."

Marie was concerned that I hadn't been checked out and suggested we do so. She asked me to get checked out a few times, and I refused. She asked the nurse, and he said it was up to me and that, minimally, I needed to have my heart checked out after what had happened. I told her I would do that in the coming days. I wanted to stay until the family arrived. The social worker informed us that the family members would be traveling a distance and would not arrive until later that night.

The nurse informed us around 7:30 p.m. that they were going to be moving the body, and we needed to leave the room. It seemed so impersonal. Within a few minutes, Marie received a call from the detectives stating they were able to locate the car, and if I wanted to get my purse, I needed to go over there immediately. We did that.

Since James was being removed from the room, we decided to head home. I was exhausted, overwhelmed, and in shock, and my clothes were soaked. Marie saw me shivering and opened a couple of the hospital room drawers, looking for anything that could help me warm up. She found some socks and got me two pairs. I put both pairs on. I was wearing my bathing suit and my sundress and had no other clothes.

It was still storming. It poured all the way home. Visibility was diminished, and we were both silent—frozen with disbelief. I felt the silence in the car. It seemed strange that I had driven there with James, and the car had been filled with joy, and now there was this deep empty hole in my chest. Marie and I didn't have many words. I knew something terrible had happened, and I was frozen in shock.

We were approaching the bridge to get to my home, and Marie said, "Look at that huge rainbow in the sky." She had never seen a rainbow so bright, and neither had I. She pointed and said, "Look. It starts right over your house."

My eyes followed the rainbow, and it looked like we were entering a portal as we approached it. Then she noticed a second rainbow that was adjacent to it. I took some pictures. Once we got to my home, I hurried to get out of the damp dress and bathing suit, and we sat for a little before Marie headed home.

I woke up the next day and was looking out the back window when a palm tree, maybe twelve feet tall, just fell forward shortly after 8:00 a.m. in the morning. It was eerie. It knocked over the Saint Francis statue that was standing over the spot where Pepper was buried. I watched from the glass doors, and it occurred to me that the tree fell over exactly the way James had. He had fallen face forward, and his entire body had seemed statuesque. It was very strange. The tree was uprooted, and the bottom of the tree did not look dead to me. Out of the blue and for no reason, it just fell.

I believe that it was James's way of reaching me. Maybe the fact that the tree wasn't dead was him saying, I *have fallen over, but I am not dead.* Maybe it fell over Pepper to let me know he was with her and there was no reason to worry. He was okay. I knew then and now that he was with me.

One day I will find the right words
and they will be simple

—Jack Kerouac

Rainbow over Gandy Bridge

Second image of rainbow over Gandy Bridge

Third image of rainbow over Tampa Bay

Fallen tree

Chapter 12

Coping

....

It is my birthright to live fully and freely.
I give to life exactly what I want life to
Give to me. I am glad to be alive.
I Love Life.

—Louise Hay

July 23, 2018

There is a process of unfolding that has been happening in the past weeks since the accident.

That first week I spent most of the weekend on the couch, riding the waves of anxiety and fear, reliving the events of June 24, 2018, in my mind. The daily thunderstorms and lightning leave me shaking with fear. I have had many panic attacks. The images play over and over in a loop. I have no control over it. I also have an overwhelming feeling of survivor's guilt. I keep asking why it was not me instead. I have many moments where I feel my life is not as valuable as James's. I know I cannot escape the dread inside of me, and I can't imagine how I will be able to go on living with it. In addition to the constant pressure in my brain, I see lights flashing in front of me, sometimes between my eyebrows and sometimes slightly to my right or above my forehead. This happens all day long.

My friends banded around me. Marie sent me an article with the side effects of being struck by lightning and urged me to get checked out by a cardiologist and neurologist. Still not feeling worthy enough of being checked out, I hesitated.

Maureen came over on Monday, June 25, 2018, to visit with me with me. She's experienced similar trauma and wanted to give me insight about the gamut of emotions that were going to flood through my being. Maureen shared that it would take a long time, but the images would go away eventually, or they would be there and would not have the same emotional intensity they had now. A lot of what she shared helped me to feel the ground under my feet again.

On Tuesday, the night after she was over, we were having a conversation on the phone, and I said to her that I was experiencing brain fogginess. I could not think of what to say to complete my sentences.

She responded, "Karen you are normally a very articulate person. I noticed you were slow in putting your sentences together yesterday when I came over to visit with you."

I started noticing that I was not remembering things, random things. The immediate effect after the accident was tingling in my feet and lower legs for the first forty-eight hours. This was when I decided to go see a neurologist. I contacted my health insurance and got a referral to a neurologist close to where I live. Other immediate symptoms included starting to tell a story and forgetting what I was talking about. I have been experiencing issue where my words come out incorrectly. I would be thinking one word, and something totally different would come out. I would go into a room and forget what I was going in there for. I would stand and space out randomly. I've been documenting my symptoms so that I can share it with my doctors. On Friday, June 29, 2018, I experienced tingling in my left hand and lower arm.

Immediately following the accident, I took three days off work. On Thursday and Friday while working from home, I struggled to recall basic tasks. I could not concentrate and found myself calling my coworker and asking him to walk me through a maintenance task I normally completed without issues.

In the next week, I saw my cardiologist, and my EKG was normal. My neurology appointment was followed by an MRI scan on June 29. The radiologist informed me immediately after the scan that he was going to contact my neurologist to request that we do a follow-up MRI with contrast on Monday, June 30, 2018. He explained that he had seen something he wanted to clear up. He explained that I would be getting a call and would need to be available to come in immediately.

I went along with whatever they asked me to do. I couldn't focus on my health. I was still in shock and disbelief. I woke up exhausted every day. I often immediately went back to sleep.

I scheduled a visit with Dr. Giusti, my primary care doctor, and I was so excited to see her. She had been very supportive of me in the last year with all the life changes I'd experienced. I was impressed by the way she connected with me on a heart level. She never forgot the details of my health and my life. She was kind and comforting and had good discernment about my symptoms. She mentioned that my symptoms were mostly consistent with anxiety, and she gave me a prescription to help relieve the intensity of my anxiety.

I was at the diagnostic clinic getting the MRI with contrast as requested after my first MRI. I waited in the waiting room between scans, since the radiologist wanted to review the results and determine whether he would need additional views. In the meantime, the technician noticed there were specific views requested by my neurologist. After getting the specific views, I waited in the waiting room while the technologist contacted the doctor (per his request) with the findings and the information regarding the specific views that were requested. As a result, the process was drawn out even more. I'd arrived around 10:00 a.m. and ended up being there all afternoon until 4:00 p.m. I was patient. I felt overwhelmed with the loss of James. I couldn't care less why they were getting specific views. Something was happening inside of me, and I wasn't able to explain it in words. I'd been changed internally by this event in a way that was incomprehensible.

I spent a lot of time in the waiting room in between capturing various views. Usually, waiting in doctors' offices or waiting rooms makes me very anxious. But on this day, my underlying anxiety was not related to sitting in the waiting room. It was just there. It had been there since June 24. An underlying feeling of dread came with it. This accompanied the replaying of all the moments that followed that initial moment when I saw that flash of lightning in my peripheral vision to the right of my head. I felt frozen inside. The dread stopped me in my tracks. It had been a reminder of the images I saw and the pain that would probably never leave me.

It's hard to breathe in an out of this. My heart is broken. I couldn't save him; this hurts so badly. I don't want to be here. I am not up to participating in the human experience anymore. It is difficult to be with myself. This is the worst experience I have ever had. How do I live with this volcano that is erupting inside of me?

While sitting there in the waiting room, I looked up for a second and noticed there was a lady who was worried and distraught across from me. She was deep in thought, just as I had been. Our eyes met, and I couldn't help but notice the despair on her face. I asked her how she was doing. She shared that she'd just learned that she had a brain aneurism. I leaned in to listen to her. I could see and feel the dread she was feeling. Her eyes filled with tears as she shared that she was just on vacation and learned this. As a result, she was here until there was additional information and was unable to fly back up to the northeast.

I got up and moved to the other side and sat next to her. I put my arms around her, and we hugged. I shared why I was there, and she said to me that there was a reason why I'd survived. I felt we were experiencing different versions of the same pain. Giving her a hug and crying together gave me an immediate sense of relief. I felt peace wash over me. A glimmer of hope crept into my heart. I am not sure what it meant, but in that moment, I felt a sense of comfort. And I realized that these were the best moments I'd experienced since the accident on the beach.

I left the office feeling lighter. I got this idea in my head that, if I could reach out to others with kindness and compassion, then I might be able to recover from this deep sense of darkness lingering within me.

The next day, the neurologist called around 10:00 a.m. and asked if I could come in at 2:30 p.m. Within ten minutes, his office called back and asked me to come in at 12:30 p.m. It was around 11:00 am. I informed my manager what was going on and logged of off work.

I sat in front of the doctor, and he explained and showed me that there was a lesion of scarring on my right brain. He explained that he was referring me to a neurosurgeon based on the findings of the radiologist, who specifically mentioned the concern of a neoplasm.

However, my neurologist also showed me and gave me a copy of his research. In this study, a baby was struck by lightning on the right side of her brain while sleeping, and she had a similar lesion on her right brain. He informed me that she'd grown up to be fine.

The good news was that he also found a baseline brain scan I took in 2017, and the results were normal. He mentioned that, if I had a neoplasm, this would have most likely showed up on the MRI of my brain that was done in 2017. I believe my original brain scan had been due to a concern about my pituitary gland. It was normal.

My neurologist stated we needed to rule things out. He mentioned that although they needed to rule out a neoplasm, he was hopeful because my MRI results were similar to that of the baby. This meant that the findings were most likely tied to having been struck by lightning. He reiterated that the baby had grown up to be fine, with good cognitive abilities.

I listened and followed up with scheduling an appointment with the neurosurgeon. Honestly, I was just going through the motions, because this was worrying Marie and Maureen more that it was me.

My neurologist also suggested that I see a psychiatrist. I did not follow up on this. After a few days, my neurologist followed up with a phone call to me. He urged me strongly to set up the appointment with the psychiatrist, since I continued to have symptoms, and the doctors needed to differentiate whether my symptoms were due to the trauma or a physiological result of the electrical impact on my brain and body. He wanted me to see a psychiatrist, since they needed to determine how much of my symptoms were related to PTSD and how much was related to the scarring on my brain.

My neurologist, Dr. Reddy, suggested someone who was highly trained, and I reluctantly scheduled the appointment with the psychiatrist. I continued to have visits with my psychologist, Dr. Toms.

August 17, 2018

In my session today, I asked Dr. Toms to help me deal with my fear of being judged by others in the coming sessions. My homework was to write down when judgment came up for me whether it was from others or from myself. I wrote this:

> The part of me that is having trouble being present is the part of me that feels like it is my fault that James lost his life. This part of me believes that, if I'd never met him, he may still be alive. Dr. Toms shared that there are laws of nature, and if we are on the path when those specific forces are prevalent, then we interact with those forces. I'm judging myself for not having better judgment on June 24, 2018. I am judging myself because, at the time, I did not say, "Let's get off the beach and find shelter." And I know that the longer I hold on to this judgment of what I should have done, the longer it will take to fully find peace within myself about losing James and the intensity of all I am feeling and experiencing as I accept this really happened. The reality is that I cannot escape to other thoughts or any other ideas in my mind because I am in this fully. I am living it fully. There is no other option but to be with all my experience fully. I know all the loss that has occurred.

I was being fully present in the moment with the interaction with James, as he was being fully present with me. I am certain of one thing—if I continue to be critical of myself about what I "should" have done, I will continue to be stuck in those memories. I am missing out on current moments when I am in mind being critical of myself. By being critical of myself, I create conditions that support a fatigued mental state of mind—the cause of which is the amount of time I spend focusing on critical energy during my day. This awareness helps me with consciously acknowledging when I am being critical and choosing a different mental state. This is really challenging and almost impossible right now.

I can't seem to connect the moments of us just walking and chatting and looking at each other to the moments following when I first felt the electricity going through my body and then witnessing it also happening to him. This is where I'm stuck—where I'm still in disbelief or denial or whatever. It's the part of me that does not want to accept that this accident happened. There is a part of me that reassures me, saying, *Try to bring yourself back to the fun, happy moments you both experienced. That's what he would want you to do. Be here* now. *Be here, Karen. This is life, nothing else.* This part of me is not making sense to me right now. I am being present with this deep sense of sadness and all the emotions I am experiencing. This is all I can do.

After I shared this with Dr. Toms on August 31, 2018, he left me with these words: "You have to continue his legacy in your life. He continues to live through you. He just touched you so profoundly. I want you to continue that spirit that you both shared for that short period of time. Kindness, gentleness, love, and peace are the wonderful traits you have. Rules don't matter. I want you to get your fighting spirit back.

"Just turn it loose. Let the universe take you where you're supposed to go."

August 20, 2018

I saw the neurosurgeon today. He mentioned that the MRI of my brain shows inflammation, and he is certain that it resulted from the electrical impact of the lightning strike. This is not a neoplasm. He asked about my symptoms.

I mentioned my main symptoms: I have pressure on the right side of my brain. I am constantly fatigued, and I wake up exhausted in the morning. I have difficulty concentrating, and my memory has been impacted. I start telling a story and then forget what I was saying midsentence. I am not able to multitask at work. And if I am under pressure to do several tasks, my mind goes blank, and I completely forget how to accomplish the task at hand. I hit a brick wall, and my mind goes blank. I often space out.

The neurosurgeon cautioned me about the possibility of having seizures or a stroke. I was now overwhelmed with fear about having a stroke, since my dad had three strokes last year. The neurosurgeon reiterated over and over that it was important for me to not push myself. He wanted to see me again in October after the three-month follow-up MRIs were completed.

August 24, 2018

I saw the neurologist today. I am going to be on medical leave for two months. I've been struggling at work. I am unable to comprehend and have issues recalling information. I am not able to concentrate. There is so much pressure on the right side of my brain. I was hoping to be able to work so I could get my mind off the repetitive replaying of images of the accident. It was helpful to see the psychiatrist.

Things started to make sense after listening to all he shared with me. He provided a copy of the research he'd obtained from the University of Chicago that was done to determine the effects of lightning strikes on people. Dr. Ahmed explained that the trauma I'd experienced might be resulting in cognitive impairment. The trauma had resulted in psychological impairment but may be causing the cognitive issues I was experiencing, such as issues with processing speed, concentration problems, and memory loss and confusion.

He shared results from the research study, showing that there were psychological effects, as well as cognitive effects after the electrical impact of being struck by lightning. He explained that the symptoms I was experiencing were what he typically saw in patients with traumatic brain injury, which are considered to be PTSD, and informed me that, if we could minimize the PTSD, we could safely ascertain how much of my symptoms were physiological.

I have been taking a couple prescriptions to minimize my PTSD symptoms. Even though I was hesitant to go see the psychiatrist, I am grateful that I followed through. He is highly educated and was very prepared.

September 1, 2018

I have been taking the meds, and I'm holding on. I draw the blinds and hunker down on my couch daily when the daily thunderstorms come through, and I start shaking and crying uncontrollably. I am exhausted all the time. The pressure in the right side of my brain never leaves. I sleep more than I'm awake. I sleep between twelve to sixteen hours a day.

I am heading to New York City tomorrow. I am attending the Rise Sister Rise workshop with Rebecca Campbell. This trip was planned earlier this year in February, and Marie and I had intended to attend the workshop together. She's not able to attend the workshop.

I felt strongly that I needed to be at this workshop, since Rebecca Campbell's work has been key to my healing process in the last year. In the last week since I have been home from work, I've been doing the Joe Dispenza's meditations several hours a day. These meditations include "Reconditioning the Body to a New Mind," "Meditations for Breaking the Habit of Being Yourself," and "The Pineal Gland Tuning Meditation." It is when I am meditating that I capture a glimmer of peace. I spend time with friends and family and laugh as much as possible.

I have noticed a pattern with my state of anxiety and fear. The fearful thoughts creep in. I see the events of June 24, 2018, playing out slowly. It rises like a volcano, and fear erupts inside of me. The only thing I can do is to be present with it. It is unbearable. I breathe in an out. Mostly, I am debilitated on the couch or on my bed. I hide out, and I ride it out, knowing that thoughts are part of the process where I become overcome by fear. I ride it to a peak, trying to remember to breathe. I cry. I lose my desire to live. I often have trouble breathing and feel tightness in my chest. Sometimes I feel my stomach turn into knots. I allow it because I also know that I can't escape it. I try to remember to breathe. I cry uncontrollably. Sooner or later, it peaks, and then it subsides.

I believe in the power of my body's innate self-healing, and I am convinced that I got a second chance at life so I can make a positive impact on life. I don't know what that is. I am open to discovering it. I choose to start by being a positive influence every day. This is my small contribution. I purchased the DVD *Heal* and have listened to the books *Evolve Your Brain* and *Breaking the Habit of Being Yourself* by Dr. Joe Dispenza.

September 4, 2018

After a meditation, I shared with the group. When the session ended, Sarah approached me and mentioned that she was a medium and felt that James had crossed over before I shared. He wanted her to tell me everything was going to be okay—to tell me that he loves me and to tell me that I am a strong warrior and I am brave. She mentioned he kept saying, "Tell her I love her."

I was also approached by another participant who said he'd said, "Tell her I have great hair."

I laughed hysterically. He really does have great hair!

September 5, 2018

After a meditation, we were given time to write a letter to ourselves from the great mother. This is my letter:

> My darling daughter,
>
> I want you to know you are the embodiment of love. You are the essence of all that is kind and pure and gentle. I am expressing all that is gentle through you. When you need to be guided by me, be still and breathe in deeply. You too are a mother. You are birthing so much into this world, and you are creating through nurturance and love. Crawl into my arms and lay your head against my bosom.
>
> Whenever you are weary, you needn't be fearful or worried that you are alone or that you don't belong. You belong. You are in my heart and you are of me and from me. You are going to heal your brain and body completely in a short space of time.
>
> James's spirit will continue to live and express through you. Know that you are him, and he is you, and you have loved each other throughout time.

You chose to have this journey together to help each
other with your growth—the growth of your soul.
He has offered to guide you, so call on him. Talk
to him all the time. Look to the stars for answers—
literally and as you both did through astrology.
Look for signs. He will respond. He is with you.
The answers will indeed reveal themselves.

You must continue to love and nurture your
heart and spirit first, and you will have the guidance
of the entire universe. Be still and know that I am
here with you, in you, and I love you, my child.

Your Great Mother

Chapter 13

Connecting

· ·

Maybe for you there's one thousand
tomorrows, or three thousand, or
ten, so much time you can bathe
in it, roll around it, let it slide like
coins through your fingers. So much
time you can waste it. But for some
of us there's only today. And the
truth is, you never really know.

—Lauren Oliver

January 19, 2019

The past months have been a process of discovery and understanding about how my life has changed as a result of the accident on June 24, 2018. I've learned that I had a stroke on the right side of my brain and sustained permanent neurological deficits.

I performed the neurofunction test on November 27, 2018 and November 28, 2018, and received the report approximately one month later. The neurofunction test results show that I've "sustained residual cognitive deficits."

Based on the neuropsychological evaluation performed by Dr. Donnell, "Language weaknesses were noted in confrontation naming and semantic fluency though phonemic fluency, word knowledge, and verbal abstract reasoning were intact. Data are consistent with right frontoparietal involvement given left sided sensory/motor deficits and visual spatial weakness as well as diffuse effects given slowed processing speed and attentional weakness. She also evidenced difficulty with language abilities (e.g. naming and semantic fluency) which may implicate left temporal involvement. It is highly likely that she will continue to experience additional cognitive improvement. Neuropsychological re-evaluation is recommended approximately 12 months post-injury."

In the meantime, I returned to work on November 2, 2018, and continued to experience pressure on the right side of my brain, as well as a flashing light between my eyebrows, sometimes above my eyes or slightly off my peripheral vision. This occurred periodically throughout the day—every day. At first my neurologist suspected that my symptoms were consistent with migraines, and I've been taking a medication for migraines for the last three months. However, the symptoms have not subsided. The pressure in my brain is present when I have stressful days or if I'm mentally exhausted after my workday. The flashes of light are not consistent with the head pressure I've experienced. Even though I've tried to pinpoint the cause of the flashes of light, I am not able to correlate the light to any specific scenario or occurrence.

In the last week, I have seen two neuropathologists who specialize in retina and glaucoma, and all seems to be fine with my eye health, as well as the nerves associated with my vision. There is a follow-up appointment in three months to determine whether the issue has resolved itself and whether my vision is getting better, getting worse, or staying the same.

I am following through with all recommendations my doctors have made and continue to visit specialist after specialist and follow the medical protocol. I've been lucky to be treated by a team of highly skilled doctors who are very talented and attentive to my situation.

I was sitting in front of Dr. Allison Donnell as she shared the results of my neurofunction test, when she informed me that there was a study done by the University of Chicago about the effects of lightning strikes on individuals and that she worked with many of those patients. This was the study that Dr. Ahmed had referenced earlier when I'd first seen him. He'd then referred me to Dr. Donnell to perform a neurofunction test.

I am grateful and delighted that I've been able to be in the care of Dr. Donnell. I know I am in good hands. I expressed to her that I'd reluctantly seen the psychiatrist Dr. Ahmed down the hall, whom I was referred to by my neurologist, Dr. Reddy, after the accident, and had only done so because the neurologist needed to be able to differentiate between my physiological and trauma-related symptoms resulting from lightning injury. At my first visit, Dr. Ahmed shared the study with me. I was impressed that he had taken the time to research the effects of lightning strikes on individuals before I came into his office. He informed me immediately that, even though this was my first visit with him, he was receiving information that I had PTSD, which typically took months to diagnose. Based on his suggestions and medical protocol, I felt confident that he could help me, and I concluded that he was an expert psychiatrist.

My heart has not been focused on my health. I've left that to the medical professionals. They've done a wonderful job of evaluating my symptoms and treating me accordingly. My heart is in need of understanding. I have been questioning *why* every day. I yearn to understand the deeper meaning of this experience. In my heart, I know that there is a spiritual meaning for every situation, circumstance, or condition. And I know I am going to get the answers if only I pay attention and go with the flow of life.

I meet Michael Brady, who is a karmic astrological life coach who specializes in past-life healing locally. Michael attained his BS in psychology and MA in clinical developmental psychology. In our discussions about the things I've experienced, I share with him that I saw an aura over Ace (the cat) in the middle of the night, and it was moving. I immediately felt like James was present. Ace was lying on the right side of my body around my leg. Then Ace got up and came over and snuggled up into my arm in a way that my arm was over his head. Ace's body trembled, and I felt his brain trembling. To me, it meant that James was trying to connect with me to say that he is aware that he was struck by lightning.

Michael mentioned that it seemed like James was hanging around—maybe to make sure I'm okay. He suggested that maybe James as worried about me because I had seen him transition like he did.

I am asked if I am ready to let him move on. I am. Michael urges me to connect with James so we can both have a sense of closure, and I can move forward. In the beginning of the recording, the transcript of which I'll share here, we are talking about lots of spiritual concepts.

When I first met Michael, he gave me a copy of my astrological chart and explained what it meant. In our second meeting, we connected with James, and I recorded the session with Michael's permission, with the intent of sharing it in my writing. Before connecting with James, our discussion entails many spiritual concepts, and we talk about my purpose here on earth from an astrological perspective. I share from the recording below, recorded on December 26, 2018:

> Michael. The meridian system, like the neural system in the body has the voluntary and the involuntary part of the neural system. In biofeedback, the only thing that is equally burned into both parts of your neural system, the voluntary and involuntary neural system, is breathing. So, at the age of three, when you can understand the words, and I can say to you, "Now I want you to hold your breath, Karen, for ten for me. Take a big breath and hold it!" you literally operate your lungs through a different wiring system than you did before I said that to you. When you are breathing spontaneously, you are breathing from the autonomic, the involuntary part of the neural system. But when you take control from your

consciousness, you switch wiring and operate your lungs from your own control. At three years old, once you understand the language, I can just tell you to switch, and it works. You don't have to practice; it is just burned into both sides of your neural system. Everything that your body does—your digestion, your heartbeat, your pulse rate, your brain speed, all kinds of things—are equally wired in both systems, but they are not imprinted into both. So, biofeedback can isolate a thing that is equally wired and burn it into your voluntary control.

For instance, let's say that you have an elevated pulse rate. Your pulse is at 100, and it is a problem. Your blood pressure is okay, but your pulse rate is hovering around 100 when you really want it to be at 80. You can come to me as a person who trains in biofeedback, and I would simply sit you in a chair like this. And I would wire your pulse and put a contact on you that would monitor your pulse rate from your wrist, and it would be wired to a light that would blink in sync with your pulse rate. Then you could literally see your pulse rate with your eyes. Right? Through the light blinking.

Karen. Right

Michael. Biofeedback is teaching you how to switch from your involuntary neural system to your voluntary neural system around your pulse rate or your heart rate. Getting started, I would have you look at the light blinking and say, "I want you to just stare at the light while you are relaxed, and I want you to take some deep breaths and keep watching the light." While doing this, I would ask you to think about the light slowing down, blinking at a slower rate. And over time, by thinking while you watch the light—this is the biofeedback loop—your brain will take the involuntary wiring operating your pulse rate and switch it over to your voluntary wiring because you are looking at your pulse rate and you are saying, *I want it to slow down*. It will begin slowing down.

Then, I'll practice that with you for a while—however often it takes or how much it takes until you can do it without the light. I would test that by having you close your eyes while you are wired and the light's here. I would have you breathe fast or get up and walk around so your pulse rate increases. Then I would check that, and then I would rewire you. Now, I would have you close your eyes, instead of watching the light. I would ask you to just think about slowing down your pulse rate while you are breathing, and I would watch the light. And I would see if the light slowed down with your eyes closed.

If the light slowed down with your eyes closed, I don't need to hook you up anymore. In effect, you have now wired and burned into control of your pulse rate in both your involuntary and your voluntary neural system. I've read that the meridians are just like the neural body system, in that they in themselves are cross connected with your nervous system. When you close your eyes and you use your third eye, which is your energy eye—his third eye that we perceive in our forehead, that's a real space; that's a real eye—it's seeing energy like your eyes see light. Except that most people can't see anything else other than the visible light spectrum with their physical eyes.

But we are wired. Both systems are wired, and when you close your eyes and channel that purple light, that's not your imagination. You are literally pulling that band of energy in the invisible range from the ethers, from everything around you into your body when you use your third eye.

There are healers who see auric energy—light you cannot see with your eyes open. You can train yourself to see ethereal energy—color—the same way that you see external light being color. You can crisscross. I got excited about wanting to experience seeing auric energy when I was learning to channel energy in a circle of people years ago.

Karen. That's out the door.

Michael. Something new showed up, and I wanted to try out the new bicycle type of thing. And that childlike energy is good for you, too, by the way.

Karen. Oh, yeah.

Michael. Using things that are unconsciously executed by your unconscious mind is done in a diffusional way—what we normally call a relaxed, dispersing, easy way. If you get too tight on either end, it knocks you over into your conscious neural system and your conscious mind. It all vanishes again. If it doesn't serve me after I have the thrill of it, I don't pursue it. Just the consciousness of it, and the childlike enthusiasm or longing, which overcomes fear, anger, frustration, and all those other emotions that would counter the occurrence of something gets replaced by that childhood longing I called it. And if you can want something and long for it in a childlike way, which means you will obsessively think about it too in the spaces, you're just walking around waiting for the right thing to show up. *Boom*! It tends to happen spontaneously, which means unintentionally, when you least expect it—when you are not trying to do it, which also tends to go with how these things show up. You've got to learn how to be in that sweet spot where you are not too tight and you are not too loose with your consciousness present, to functionally do these kinds of things intentionally in your life.

Karen. That does help. That makes sense with understanding. I knew it was him once I saw the aura over the cat because it was moving. It was around his face, and then it was hovering.

Michael. My guess is that he walked in, into the cat for a bit, or he reached through the cat to you.

Karen. Well, and once the cat got up and came over, snuggled up in my arm in a way that my hand was over his head, then his body trembled. Then when the brain started feeling the quivering—shaking—that's exactly how it felt [when the electricity from the lightning was going through my brain]. So, then I knew he was saying, "I'm aware. This is how it felt for me too. And I'm aware of it." Poor cat. I hope the cat is okay.

Michael. Cats and dogs are fine. They have been channeling stuff for us for eons.

Karen. Okay

Michael. There is a theory—I'll call it a theory—that Gaia is a word for earth, is the energy. The spiritual word for earth. In the sense that Gaia is a conscious entity.

Karen. She is, yes.

Michael. Not water and dirt.

Karen. Yes absolutely. I believe that.

Michael. Kind of like the planet in *Avatar*. They are using the concept of Gaia in that movie.

Karen. Yes, absolutely.

Michael. Now human beings, we tend to believe that we are capable of existing beyond the earth. Everything on earth belongs to earth, comes from earth. Earth is the creator of everything that is part of its domain—Gaia's domain. We tend to believe; I don't know if this is arrogant or not—

Karen, *laughs out loud.*

Michael. We tend to believe.

Karen, *laughing.* That we are going to go to Mars or the moon. (*Now laughs hysterically.*)

Michael. Everything—horses and whales and plants and rocks, everything else that we can name on the planet—isn't capable of existing independently of Gaia. They are extensions of Gaia. That brings into the whole idea of ancient aliens and that our species got messed with in the first place. We may have been kind of genetically mutated from an indigenous life form to what we now call human beings.

Karen. Huh.

Michael. Now that's way beyond the Bible story.

Karen. Right. (*Laughs.*) But I am more inclined to believe that one actually.

Both laugh out loud.

Michael. Yes. I am too—exactly! And I don't think anything isn't truth. Okay? Truth isn't one thing. It has layers of complexity—from simple to complex. It's multifaceted, kind of like a diamond. That means it has levels and aspects to it.

Karen. Right.

Michael. If a five-year-old asked you, "Mommy, where do babies come from?" and you gave the truthful answer, it would be a different language set. It would be simpler than what you would give an eighteen-year-old or a twenty-year-old, but not a fairy tale. That same child at twenty would say, "Why did you tell me that when I was five? That wasn't the whole story. Now you're telling me about sex, death, and rock 'n' Roll.

"Yes, but you weren't capable of understanding at five years old what you understand about it now."

So, truth isn't one thing. It has layers of complexity—from simple to complex. With that model of reality, there is no such thing as nontruth. There are just versions of truth. And some are simpler, and some are more complex. But they are all related to the same thing and they are all versions of an explanation of the same thing.

The fact is that, while we are on this plane, in a body, human beings can never comprehend the wholeness of truth. As far as we can tell, at least, not so far—from our own examination of things—it doesn't look like that is plausible. So, we are always going to have less than the whole package while we are here—which means all of it is in some form an approximation. Even the best explanations are still going to be less than perfect. Which frustrates us, but?

Karen. Right!

Michael. And in that model of reality, there is no such thing as one truth. There are just versions of truth and some are simpler, and some are more complex. But they are all related to the same thing, and they are all versions of an explanation of the same thing. The fact is that, when we are on this plane in a body, humans can never comprehend the wholeness of truth as far as we can tell. From the examination of our own selves, it doesn't look like that is plausible. So, we are always going to have less than the whole package while we are here—which means, all of it is some form of an approximation. Even the best explanations are still going to be less than perfect, which frustrates us. But nonetheless, those are the conditions of the earth plane as far as I can tell. At any rate, the energy that you are perceiving him through is auric energy. And it's very real what's been happening with the cat. In my opinion, he has been hanging around you ever since he left his body. Now, you just told me, clarified for me that he is not confused about if he is in body or if he is out of body. He knows he is dead.

Karen. Yeah.

Michael. So that says, he's not hanging around because he doesn't know it's time to go. He's hanging around for some other reason. I think the other reason he has been hanging around is you.

Karen. Okay.

Michael. Because you and he were in the beginning of a relationship. You were hovering around the drain with each other.

Karen. Right, right.

Michael. And *bam*! Suddenly, things got interrupted very abruptly. And there is a sense of closure that needs to occur for both you and him— especially for you, being the one still left in body— so that you could move forward without it being something undone, uncompleted, dragging along behind you.

Karen. Right.

Michael. So I think he knew that instantly when he came out of his body.

Karen. He did?

Michael. You know, because we know much more out of body than we do in body. And I am sure that he got in touch with his connection with you karmically when he came out of body—that this wasn't the first time you guys ever met.

Karen. Right. It truly felt like we knew each other for a thousand years.

Michael. And I don't think that the fact that this experience happened with you both together was an accident. So, hindsight, which is the only time when we are clear about, is that you and James set this up from the beginning before you came in.

Karen. Did I tell you about Danny, his best friend?

Michael. No I don't think you did.

Karen. Okay, so Danny and I are now in a relationship. And I was telling the other lady (referring to Yasmirys who does Reiki and Yoga) about that. Initially, when this happened, Danny and James came to my home the same day when he installed my sink.

Michael. Right.

Karen. Danny and I were standing there talking while he was working. When he was done installing the sink, he demonstrated to me that that your sink is working—showed me that there aren't any leaks. I went into the bathroom, and I don't know what happened. I felt like *pshhhhheeeeew*— like energetically something happened. Prior to that moment, I didn't pay any attention to him. He was doing his work. His friend was talking to me.

Michael. Right

Karen. They work together. They are best friends, and they are roommates as well. So Danny observed it. Danny told me about it after—the day after [the accident]. The night [of the accident], when I came home, I got Danny's number from Marie. She suggested I contact him to share what happened.

Michael. Yes

Karen. I said I was at the beach with James and asked if Danny had heard what happened. He decided to stop by after work the next day. We talked. It was sad, you know. (*Pauses and catches her breath.*) Now I'm desperate to know more about James because it feels like the rug has been pulled out from under my feet, and I don't know what happened. So, Danny is grieving. I'm grieving. There is this huge void for both of us. I invite him over to dinner. He comes over, and we talk about James. We talk about their stories—things like, you know, James was like, "How does garlic taste? Apparently, it is good for your body." They were doing some sort of cleanse or something.

Danny said, "Well, why don't you just eat it?"

And he watched him (*laughing out loud*) and laughed while James ate the garlic.

They were little stories that made me laugh and made me feel good about knowing more about him and what they did and how they interacted. They cooked together. Just silly things like that. Danny and I got closer.

Michael. Right. That was almost guaranteed. In psychology, that was almost guaranteed, and then karmically it was also guaranteed.

Karen. It was set up.

Michael. I am starting to see that there is a triangle here.

Karen. It was set up. Yasmirys said it was the triangle.

James used to tell me every preacher told him he was the reincarnation of Jesus. And my God, when he started bringing that up, I said, "Really? Are you serious?" I said, "I believe in science." I knew there was something behind this, why I had to … (*Voice trails off.*) Jesus is bringing me back to him is what … (*laughing*) I've concluded. But now, Yasmirys said to me that you three are in a contract together.

Michael. Yeah.

Karen. We have been great. My family just met him on Sunday. His parents invited me. He is going up to Tennessee today. They invited me to come out, but it's just a little too overwhelming for me to do all this all at once. I am working on figuring it out.

Michael. Yeah, yeah, exactly. You should do that for yourself first.

Karen. And, hmmmm. But everything is wonderful with him, so, you know.

Michael. Well good. That's great to hear.

Karen. You know … I don't understand, it was … Like you said, sometimes it's just easy. I've struggled with … you know my ex-husband. I married him twice, and there was just so much stuff and heaviness around our relationship. And then … Now, I decide to wake up and be present, and I'm writing about it this whole year. I started writing in January—writing this book—and I said, *Let me just see what happens. I have no plans.* And here we are.

Michael. There is a line in the Bible, in the New Testament as Jesus goes into Jerusalem on the donkey on Good Friday—no Palm Sunday. I'm Roman Catholic. I should know this!

Karen. Yeah, I was raised Roman Catholic too.

Michael. He turns, and he says to someone, "Go find me a man carrying a jug of water." In Jesus's time, Jews, Romans, Greeks, whoever—men did not tote water. That was a woman's job, and things were very compartmentalized socially, ethically across the board like that. So, he was talking to somebody like today saying, like, "Go find me a girl who has a pink elephant as a pet and bring her to me." What's he talking about?

Karen. It's almost the impossible. Men don't do that.

Michael – Men don't do that! If you look at astrology, one of the symbols of Aquarius, the sign of Aquarius is a person carrying, holding a jug of water, carrying a jug of water, and water is pouring forth from the jug. Okay, that is a symbol of the astrological sign of Aquarius—a person carrying a jug of water. So, in my opinion, Jesus was prophesying the Age of Aquarius. He was talking about the Age of Aquarius that we are in the beginning of now. Every two thousand years. I think Jesus recognized, because I don't think he was just a carpenter. If anything, he was a construction worker. Okay. The amount of wood in Galilee couldn't support a carpenter for ten minutes. So, things weren't made of wood very much back in Galilee; they were made of stone. King Herod built a palace within walking distance of Nazareth during Jesus's lifetime growing up. Joseph wasn't a carpenter. He was a construction worker, and his son was probably engaged in construction work too, for a while. But Jesus was also from the line of David. There are twelve tribes of the Jews.

Karen. Uh-huh.

Michael. He was from the royal tribe, like the house of Saudi—the house of Saud. Those are the royal family members. Well, David's line was the royal family line in the Jewish culture. So, he was aristocracy. I don't care how he lived; he was aristocracy spiritually, culturally, within his own community. And a Messiah wasn't ... A magician, a healer, and a Messiah were technical job titles in that era—technical job titles. There wasn't just one magician floating around. There were many magicians floating around. They did a certain job. Healers did a certain job. Messiahs did a certain job in the Jewish culture. Moses was a messiah of the Jewish culture. It wasn't just a one-person title in the Jewish folklore or their—

Karen. And what is a messiah?

Michael. It is the person who is sent, who arises in the Jewish culture to save them from oppression—period! That's what the term means in Hebrew. John the Baptist was the messiah before he got his head cut off. Jesus was a follower of John the Baptist and took up his cause when he died. Now, what made Jesus special? Because he wasn't the only messiah floating around either; there were lots of messiahs floating around in the Jewish world. Well, not a lot, but more than one or two at a time, and they were all magicians and healers too—which are, again, like a musician, an accountant, a lawyer. It was a job title.

What made Jesus special was, as a healer, he healed for free. Nobody did that. John the Baptist didn't heal for free. They had to have a living. These people—again, these are their job titles okay. So, when you came to John the Baptist and asked him to heal you from something, you offered him alms. You gave him money or something in trade, and he would exercise his skill level as a healer. He would heal you, or he would do magic, whatever they would define as magic back then, things that other people can't do. He spoke about freedom from oppression as a part of what he preached, one way or another, which made him a zealot—which was a political term pertaining to oppression of Rome and the desire to be free from the Romans. And Jesus took all that up. What Jesus did that was unique in that field of messiahs, healers, and magicians was that he offered his services for free. Now imagine, one guy shows up and says, "Hey, I'll heal you. I'll do this, no charge."

Karen. Of course. He is going to stick around for two thousand years!

Michael. It was like going to the store and saying all the goods are free. Yes you are going to have a crowd at the store the first day!

Karen. You're going to be the one they praise for the next two thousand years.

Michael. And he rapidly gathered a following because of that one brilliant move of his. Now, I also believe—because we lose track of him in the Bible, from the age of twelve until thirty, approximately, thirty and the ages aren't right either—probably cause their gauging of his birth years probably isn't correct based on astrology.

Karen. (*Laughs out loud.*)

Michael. They are off by three or four years. But at any rate, in that period, at ages twelve—eleven to fifteen—in all cultures, is when girls become women. You get your period. You have a rite of passage in a lot of cultures—a rite of passage that marks you as an adult now. Okay?

Karen. Uh-huh.

Michael. And boys too. In the Jewish culture, you get circumcised at twelve to fourteen years old. They don't do it to you when you are a baby. They wait until … (*voice trails off*)

Karen. Well, that's brutal.

Michael. Yeah, well it's the ritual in Jewish culture of transitioning from childhood to adulthood. You become a man when you are circumcised. So at any rate, it's not an accident that Jesus has disappeared in his life at twelve years old because that was when he would have been sent away to be trained and educated according to his status in his culture, which is royalty. So, he was taught astrology. He was taught the mysteries. He was taught what we call extrasensory information. He was taught how to channel. He was taught Chinese medicine. He knew about meridians, however they worded that back then. That knowledge was floating around amid all cultures in what we call the healing class, the healers, the prophets.

Karen. It's universal information.

Michael. Correct, yeah—exactly! Jesus was very educated, and he probably also could read and write, which most people in those times didn't read and write. Only the priest class and the ruler class were taught to read and write—even in Hebrew culture back then. But he was probably taught to read and write, so he was an intellectual for his era. This is all very different than the idea of a poor wood carpenter.

Karen. (*Giggles out loud.*)

Michael, *laughing*. Sure. That's not really what happened. Now, the interesting thing, though, is that Jesus did not advocate overthrowing the Roman Empire. And he was more concerned with corruption within the Jewish religion itself because it was all built around temple culture. To be a good Jew, you had to show up for the holidays. To show up for the holidays, you had to sacrifice on the holidays. Animal sacrifice, okay. And you had to buy the animals in the temple in Jerusalem. And the temple in Jerusalem—and all Jewish temples are made this way—they have three layers in them. There is an outer wall or an outer perimeter, and in that first courtyard is a public arena. There would be people selling things there, such as chickens and goats and things for sacrifice. There was money changing going on in the first courtyard of the temple.

The second courtyard of the temple is where the worship occurred—where the prayers were said by the priests publicly, and the men would be isolated in one section and the women isolated in a separate section. They didn't mix them together—in church, okay.

And then the third was the holy of holies— where they had the Arch of the Covenant and which was supposedly a real magical machine and did all kinds of things. And only the priests could enter that part of the temple. Only a priest could be ever be in the presence of that Arch of the Covenant. Okay, so that was the culture of the Jewish faith. Like the Catholic Church's culture, right, you must go to Mass every Sunday, yada yada.

Karen. Umm-hmmm. Yeah, we did—*every* Sunday.

Michael. Eighty percent of the Jews were the poor; the downtrodden; the overrun, overworked, underpaid class—overworked by the oppressors, the Roman conquerors in that area. Most of them were poor. The only people in the Jewish culture that had any money were the Pharisees, which were the priests.

Karen. Okaaaay.

Michael. Who ran the temple, because all those people selling the animals for sacrifice, paid for the right to be in that part of the temple, to sell that. So the Priest made money off of the congregation buying out from sacrifice. And the Jewish tenet was that only the priest could offer the sacrifice.

You couldn't offer your own sacrifice to God— in Jesus's time. So you and I, as a normal Jewish person being called to holiday or the Sabbath, would have to scrape some money to have to go and buy something—a chicken, a goat, or something we could afford. And then we'd move into the next realm of the temple, where the worship service goes on. And we present our sacrifice to the priests because only they can offer it for us—which means that there is no way to operate, to be in connection with God, to abide by the rules of holiness outside of the temple. It had absolute control—in the material possessions! Does that sound like the Roman Catholic Church?

Karen. Oh yeah. The Vatican is its own country.

Michael. It is its own country—exactly! Yes! Like the United States is independent of everybody else in the world.

Karen. Right!

Michael. So, in Jesus's time, he was angrier with the church—his church—than he was with the Roman, although he was also pissed off that his people were being oppressed. But what he talked about most had to do with his own people. Jesus was Jewish. He only talked to Jews. He only healed Jews. He never said a word to what would be called goyim in his entire life.

Karen. And what's a goyim?

Michael. People who are not Jewish.

Karen. Okay.

Michael. A Roman, a heathen, a white person—whoever. And he probably wasn't white either. If you look at Aramaic people, in that history—

Karen. Right, right.

Michael. They were more on the dark skin side than they were on the Caucasian side.

Karen. Yes, yes, yes.

Michael. Sooo. Jesus didn't have long blond curls.

Karen. In that part of the world, if you go there—which I haven't been—but if you go there, you're right, that is what you see. You're going to see people of slightly darker complexion—olive skin.

Michael. So Jesus rode into Jerusalem on the donkey, and he said that line. I believe he knew that he didn't have a shot in hell—because the Pharisees ... You know that parable where he overturns the table of the money changers.

Karen. Uh-huh.

Michael. That's in the first courtyard of the temple. He messed with their money. He took on not the Romans but the Pharisees—the priest class of the Jewish faith. Okay?! In church, in the building! That's like attacking the Pope.

Karen. So no wonder they wanted to—

Michael. They wanted him out. They wanted him out of the way. And it's always about money, right?

Karen. Right! Even back then—even back then.

Michael. Exactly! So, he knew he had blown it or that they were going to get him one way or another. He knew that the end was coming, that he didn't have a shot, and he wasn't willing to organize a revolt. He probably knew that wouldn't work either—either within the Jewish culture or within the larger Roman culture. I mean, the Romans would've come in and slaughtered everybody. They don't care. And that's the way most of the world has worked anyway, for like five thousand years—that we know of. So, at any rate, when he said that line, I think what he was saying was that he recognized what he came and talked about, which was heaven inside ourselves, and heaven being on earth here, not somewhere up in the clouds when you are dead. What he talked about the people weren't getting.

Karen. It's not literal ... yes.

Michael. And you aren't going to get it for a thousand years, because he understood astrology. He knew what the Age of Pisces was. He knew the Age of Aquarius was supposed to be. He had ideas about the evolution of ages that you and I are talking about today. That wasn't part of his mindset. So he was saying, "What I represent is not going to take while I am here, and it's not going to take probably for the whole time I am supposed to be here." If people didn't get him then, how are they going to get it after he's gone? Because anyone who is smart like that knows that information gets distorted as it gets passed down the line.

Karen. Yes, yes, yes.

Michael. He knew that we were not going to understand what he was trying to tell us about the age "go find me a man carrying a jug of water." It was a prophecy that we wouldn't get—what Pisces really is about.

Karen. Wow, I saw the light flash in front of me right there.

Michael. Until we began the Age of Aquarius.

Karen. Now, the Age of Aquarius began?

Michael. There's an argument about that. That's a debatable issue.

Karen. Tell me.

Michael. I believe that now, at this point in this carnation, we are completely done. We are out of the space of the Age of Pisces, and we have both feet in the Age of Aquarius. That doesn't mean that the people with both feet in Aquarius have left their Piscean stuff behind them.

Karen. No, we must work it out.

Michael. Right. You can still bring your Piscean stuff into the box we'll call the Age of Aquarius, which is a lot of what's going on. But I think we are in the space, the energy, the timeframe where we're not a foot in both worlds—which is where we were born. I believe we're in the Age of Aquarius. So, the reason I am telling you all that is because I think you are the man carrying the jug of water. I think I am the man carrying the jug of water.

Karen. You know what I just thought of while you were saying all that? I didn't even think of it. I don't think of anything anymore. I stopped thinking after my brain got ... (*Laughs out loud*). But what came to me was that you said something about my Capricorn is in the unconscious house of whatever.

Michael. Twelfth house.

Karen. Twelfth house of unconscious. I studied Capricorn to some degree. I wrote a book, *Peter Crane Mountain Goat*, which hasn't been published. It was my process of understanding the mountain goat because—

Michael. Which is a symbol of Capricorn, by the way.

Karen. Another astrologer said to me that, if I wanted to understand what I embody in this lifetime, read up on mountain goats. And that led me to writing a story. I wrote a story about Peter Crane mountain goat moving his mountain goat tribe from one mountain to another. He's a baby, and after his mom is attacked by mountain lions, he sets out to move his tribe to a different mountain. Then a wise sage mountain goat helps him to get the tribe across to the mountain where the mountain lions will not be able to attack them.

So, in talking about this, I realize that mountain goats are rulers of the high country. They are the rulers of the mountains, and the twelfth house of the unconscious for me is understanding it in this physical sense. That's why I am having this experience—you and I are having this conversation.

Michael. Your job is to bring spirit down to earth—period. That is a one-line interpretation of a north node in Capricorn in the twelfth house. Your job is to bring spirit down to earth. Your job is to eventually bring spirit down to the earth.

Karen. And ground it.

Michael. And ground it, yes, and then you got struck by ... Is there anything more—

Karen. Spirit is like, "You're not going to buzz through life in your IT job. I'm going to be certain you can't do that anymore."

Michael. That's right. That's exactly right.

Karen. Because I was getting very comfortable there.

Michael. Unless you believe things are very random—stuff just happens.

Karen. No. I think, I think we live in an organized universe.

Michael. Me too, and I think its order is more complex than we could ever wrap our heads around.

Karen. We don't have the capacity to understand it.

Michael. No, not all of it—completely.

Karen. No.

Michael. Just approximations of it. And you can get a better approximation and a better approximation, but you're never going to get to the end of the box.

Karen. Yeah.

Michael. Unless you're in space, where you're in vertical time. So, when you're in trance, when you're having a meditation, when you're in special spaces that life pushes you in, yes, there are moments when we can get it. But you know what? There is no language that can adequately express whatever it is you "got."

Karen. And that's the only way I can express it—through writing. Right, are you familiar with Rumi—a poet from the thirteenth century?

Michael. Yes.

Karen. He got it, but he couldn't explain it any other way but through poetry.

Michael. And Khalil Gibran got it too.

Karen. Yes!

Michael. He was way ahead of his time. He was an Aquarian who lived and died in the Age of Pisces. He was a writer and a poet.

So you could feel it. You could experience. You could know it.

Karen. And then everything is a metaphor.

Michael. But you can't reiterate it enough, completely enough.

Karen. Yeah, and I understand for me that I can express this through my writing. When I sit down to write, it is almost like going on a quest. Let's go on. Tell me what's next. This session is going to be in my writing. Did I ask you if it's okay to put your name in there?

Michael. You did, and I told you yes. You can use my real name. It's fine.

Karen. Your full name or just your first name?

Michael. Any information about me. Yeah you can put my whole name in, and you can put my history in there. I don't care.

Karen. Okay.

Michael. I am not hiding.

Karen. I can't verbalize things right now, but when I sit down to write, it is almost like—there it goes. It takes over my fingers, and it just comes out. I light a candle, and I invite all my angels and guides and James.

Let's go on. Tell me what's the next step on this journey, because I stopped making plans at the beginning of this year. And I said I'm just going to be in the present moment with my life.

Michael. Yeah.

Karen. And here it is. (*Giggles out loud.*) Okay?

Michael. Yeah, I think you and James and—

Karen. Danny.

Michael. And Danny are all men carrying the jug of water that Jesus referred to. All of us! All of us who are self-aware and beginning the cleaning up of the Age of Pisces and the beginning of the exploration of the themes of the Age of Aquarius are the men carrying the jug of water. I don't think he was referring to one person. I think he was referring to anybody, everybody at the end of the Age of Pisces ushering in. That journey is for those of us who become self-aware and are leaning in with awareness into the Age of Aquarius. We have no choice but to look back at what the Age of Pisces was about because it is like going from high school to college. How could you start your first year of college, let's say, at the age of eighteen or the age of nineteen and not look back and compare it immediately to what you just left? And it's like apples and oranges when you go from high school to college, isn't it? Well, that's what an age shift is like from one age unit to the next. There's no way that those of us who are with awareness moving into the Age of Aquarius proactively—

Karen. Can go back to that way of thinking.

Michael. Can … not go back and review all this stuff.

Karen. Right! Right!

Michael. And in reviewing it sort out what was the nonsense and what wasn't—what was useful, what was the truth, what got distorted on a personal level.

Karen. Oh, yeah, we've got to start with ourselves.

Michael. And even if you never said a word of that to another person, it is changing us and the way that we live in ourselves, and then we rub off on other people because other people contact us. It doesn't mean you have to prophesize or to take it up as a job. Just doing what you are doing for yourself is, in fact, that work of the man carrying the jug of water. We're cleaning up Pisces, and we are clearing a path for people, other people to step into Aquarius and start to change their heads to the next frame.

Karen. And be in a space where they are operating from authenticity.

Michael. Yes, more authenticity—because you know, again, we asked for Jesus, but we got the church. So a lot of the theology we have bought for two thousand years contained distortions.

Karen. Yeah, yeah. At the core of it, it is essentially beautiful if you study it the way you did. Here is what I want to share with you next. One of the things that came up with my work with Yasmirys when I receive Reiki, bodywork, and yoga is that I have a contract with the universe to share this spiritual journey with others. She mentioned that this is my gift. She said something to the effect of, "I know it doesn't feel like it because you have been knocked down, knocked down, and knocked down again. But you are getting up because you chose this when you came in."

I told her I didn't change my name, and she mentioned that I had to change my name back to my maiden name, Maharaj.

Michael. You come from a spiritual line.

Karen. So I must go and get my name changed.

Michael. Yeah you do.

Karen. My contract with the person I was married to is done. I made a contract with the universe to publish my spiritual work, and it will only be published under my maiden name. So, this just came up because of what you were saying, and I am getting a confirmation that I need to do this.

Michael. Yeah, yeah. And you know being struck by lightning was like a necessary thing for this to work. People are always going to be interested once they know that you got struck by lightning and survived. And then she wrote a book. That's what you are here to do, to spread information—to bring spirit down to earth. You're one of the men carrying a jug of water in my opinion, on this planet right now.

Karen. And honestly, Michael, ever since I've been a child, the only thing that is important to me is my trust and connection in spirit.

Michael. In spirit, yeah.

Karen. It's the most important thing to me.

Michael. And Capricorn says that you're going to do it in a way that's palatable to the common person.

Karen. Yes. Oh yeah.

Michael. Traditional framework that allows them to hear what you are saying or accept your explanation—that's the Capricorn part. Grounded in the earth. And that's tricky stuff.

Karen. Good luck with that, right? I still don't know. Oh. Here we go. The room is changing. You see it? You feel it?

Michael. Yes, I feel it more than see it. Yeah.

Karen. But I don't have to know is what I

realize. (stating that I don't have to understand what I am feeling or seeing when I am having a spiritual experience)

Michael. No you don't!

Karen. Because it's all going to happen anyway. (*Chuckles out loud.*) I don't have to plan anything ever again. I just have to sit back and take the queues and do the things that I know I am—

Michael. Right. Pay attention as best you can to what's going on.

Karen. The nudges. I must go with those.

Michael. Invest wholeheartedly in what you choose to do.

Karen. Yes.

Michael. And then let go of the outcome.

Karen. Yeah.

Michael. Now that sounds simple, but it is tricky to pull off. It's not easy to do, but that's the mission. As well as you do that, what you came here to do will express more toward the optimal expression. We are cleaning up Pisces, correcting the record, at least personally for ourselves.

Karen. God is not out there.

Michael. It's going to rub off even if you don't talk about it, and we're opening the box. We're going, What is this Aquarius? How does this work? That's not a book written. It is an evolving lesson, like Pisces was an evolving lesson. We're the beginning explorers of the Age of Aquarius. We are figuring out what the foundational premises of the Age of Aquarius are going to be about. Functionally, while we are here and then it passes down the line. So, none of this stuff is accidental, and you being struck by lightning and surviving that. And especially with the contrast of James not surviving. That's important too. Because that makes you even more weird or special.

Karen. I'm special! (*Laughs hysterically out loud.*)

Michael. Or miraculous. Any of those will work, depending on the person who is observing that comment. Because of the contrast of he didn't make it and she did make it—

Karen. And we were standing next to each other.

Michael. You shouldn't have made it, okay?

Karen. *Noo*!

Michael. Period! That makes you special, and the curiosity about that will last the rest of your life. So, there's your hook—once you get an audience, either the book or at a hall or at a workshop.

Karen. Then I tell them what I have been realizing my whole life—that God is not outside of us. It's—

Michael. There you are, cleaning up the Age of Pisces.

Karen. The whole universe is inside us—it's inside of us. And what we must understand is that we are not reaching out for something. We are creating our lives through these eyes.

Michael. Every second of our lives is self-created. Every person is self-created.

Karen. There is so much, and I had to learn all of that as I came along and not learn it but create it.

Michael. What we are doing is we are remembering what we've already learned.

Karen. Yes.

Michael. What we've learned a thousand times along the way.

Karen. That's right, that's right. That step came first for me out of a discipline and the life that I chose to come into—the hardship of my family life. Ummm, the abandonment and all that crap from childhood, which I've worked through in so many ways—in therapy and this and that and the other.

Michael. When I was around seven to eight years old, a year or two after my mom died—and she was the only safe person in my family—I had this dream that I've carried my whole life. So I had it around eight years old, just before I turned eight. And I was in my grandparents' house, which was a three-story brownstone in Baltimore, built in the 1800s. Very narrow but very deep houses, plaster walls; they had bay windows in the front that sat out over the street.

For a kid, they were magical houses. And the bottom of the magical house, the basement—ahh—was the dark woods where the big bad wolf lived, where all the monsters came out. I mean it was a dirt floor, light bulb basement with big old coal-burning and then steam-operational heating furnaces. It was dark back there. So, I never went down in the basement. I had this dream around eight years old, when I lived in the house. I was there when I had the dream.

I dreamed that I woke up, and I went downstairs in the dark. And I was on the first floor. It was not lit. Everybody was asleep. I walked over to the bay window, and I looked out at the empty street. Then I turned around and the basement stair door was underneath the front steps that led in the front door out of the foyer. So I turned back around, and I looked, and I was drawn in the dark to the door of the basement.

I felt this compulsion, like the classic horror movies. Let's take the car. No. Let's go hide behind the chainsaw over there. That will be safe. I felt this compulsion to go toward the door. When I got to the door, I had this compulsion to open the door and walk down the steps. You know, I am eight years old, and I am like ...voodoo. I don't want to go down there with somebody half the time.

So, I stepped in, and there was a pull chain at the top. There was a bulb at the top that lit the steps and illuminated the darkness, six or eight feet into the basement. Then you'd have to pull strings as you proceeded forward. I couldn't reach half of them. They were too high. So, I never went down there by myself. But in this dream, I went down the steps, and I was compelled to go toward the furnace, which is in the back in the deepest part, where I would never go on my own. Well, I'd only been back there in the daytime with my Aunt Mary or whoever maybe once or twice. I didn't even like the place in the daytime. In this dream, I went into the darkness; it got darker and darker and darker as I got toward the back. I looked up now I was in the basement, and I could see the night sky. You know how dreams work. They are magical. Okay?

Karen. Yeah.

Michael. So the house kind of went away. But I am in the basement, and I'm seeing the night sky—after you get out of town when the lights go down and all the stars are just popping at you. There is this big wrought iron spiral staircase that's probably as wide as this room in diameter. It was black. It was wrought Iron. It was like twelve feet wide, and it got lost going up toward the night sky. I couldn't see the end of it. It reminded me of the Tower of Babel story. I had that story in my head by then.

I was compelled to step onto the spiral staircase, because I was awe struck by the night sky, and I wanted to get a better look. I wanted to get closer to the stars. I put a hand on a railing, and I started to walk up the staircase. But the further I went, suddenly, the base started wobbling. It felt like it wasn't steady and could fall over. The higher I went, the wobblier it got, the more I had to literally balance the staircase. I'm holding both railings now, somehow—you know, like you're trying to control the wobble with the railings. That was the whole dream.

I woke up the next day, remembering that I was climbing the spiral staircase into the night sky toward the stars out of the basement. I remembered that dream in my twenties when I was studying toward my bachelor's in psychology. I've dreamed it, I don't know, four to five times in my life as I've gone through it. It has come back to me until it's a very permanent conscious kind of memory. I mean all those details; I can feel myself as a child. And now, I didn't have a clue what that dream meant until I was about thirty-five. It was about, exactly about, what I was going to do with my life. Wasn't it?

Karen. Uh-huh. Something special about that dream.

Michael. It was mystical as hell as a child. It was a prophesized dream.

Karen. There is something. I had to close my eyes and be there.

Michael, *taking a deep breath*. And I was more fascinated than I was scared.

Karen. Yeah. (*Allows a long pause and then lowers voice.*) 'Cause you're coming out of the darkness, and you're taking the journey up into the wide, vast, open sky. (*Takes a deep breath.*)

There is silence for over a minute.

(*This is where Michael saw me go into trance and started to work with my unconscious mind.*)

Michael. While you are there right now, think about James. What happens when you think and you bring James to mind?

Karen. He just came. (*Clears her throat.*)

Michael. Can you feel him?

Karen. He just came onto the stairway, and he joined me.

Michael. Good.

Karen. And he is giggling.

Michael. Good.

Karen. Now we are walking up the stairs, going up into the sky. We used to love to look up at the sky—at the stars.

Michael. Have the conversation that you and he need to have with each other now, while you're there with each other.

Long pause.

Karen. He's saying, "I know you know that time is not real, and it's going to be like we weren't apart for very long when we see each other again." (*Remains silent for a long space of time.*) And he is here.

Michael. Good. Be sure to tell him what you need to say for yourself as well. Don't hold anything back. (*Allows a long pause.*) Say everything that is important for you to say to him. Feel everything.

Karen, *sobbing.*

Michael. It all belongs to you to be shared in any number of ways that you decide.

Karen. (*Continues to sob.*)

Michael. Let your heart breathe. Breathe through your heart. Let go of any density—anything stuck in your heart. Let your heart be restored, revitalized. It is your most important tool in this life. It is the most important part of your mind in this life. (*Takes a deep breath out loud.*)

Karen, *still sobbing.*

Michael. We come here to keep having the joy of rediscovery of who we are. There's a purpose in forgetting, therefore. You can't have that joy of discovery over and over unless you forget in between. (*Allows for a space of silence.*) You came here to have many important experiences of great joy and discovery. And most of them are waiting for you in front of you.

Karen. He just said that he's going to carry me through the rest of this journey on this planet. And he said I am safe with Danny, and he knows that Ace is happy with me. And he keeps nudging me to keep climbing the stairway.

Michael. Is there anything holding you back?

Karen. We're going forward. He's holding my hand—he says, because we must reach the stars. We made that promise. The whole universe is counting on us. (*Voice cracks and tears up.*) He said I know you get sad and depressed, but you're stronger than you think you are.

Michael. You're as strong as you need to be. We all are. You know what real strength is, don't you? It's a completely open heart. A completely open heart is indestructible.

Karen. He says he loves me.

Michael. Can you accept that?

Karen, *with voice cracking.* Yes

Michael. Do you feel the same way for him?

Karen. Yes.

Michael. Now, whenever you two connect with your awareness, you'll always have that feeling—that presence. There is nothing more than that. To come down here and to discover something new again—it's a rush that we can't replicate in other realms. There is something very special about the earth realm.

Karen. Yeah.

Michael. And yet we disparage it most of the time we are here.

Karen. He is showing me the light that I see as truth, and he says he's part of that. He said, "I am in you." His energy, but not like the physical him. And then he is showing me the light opening. My whole brain is opening. The light becomes brighter and brighter. We're going up further up the staircase, and he is holding me closer. The whole sky is becoming brighter with the light that is coming out of my head. So the dark sky that we were looking up at—as we were on the staircase [from] when you were telling me about your experience, and I could see all the stars in the sky—is being lit up with the light that is coming out of my head. And I don't know what that means, but I don't need to understand it.

Michael. What does it feel like?

Karen. It feels like home.

Michael. It feels like home. Doesn't that say it all? You're home now. Even while you are in a body, pretending to be Karen for a while.

Karen. And now he is showing me our hearts are intertwined. Like there's his heart and my heart, and there's a light—almost like the spark of the lightning. And that is going from heart to heart, and it looks like a DNA spiral.

Michael. Yes, ah Möbius loop. Ever heard about a Möbius strip?

Karen. No.

Michael. It's a circle that's got three dimensions, so it's got length, width, and depth. So it's kind of like a road. Except it's a circle; it's got a loop. And it is twisted in just the right way to where you're on the surface of the road, and you infinitely go around in a circle. You never reach the end of it.

Karen. Ummm-huh. He said there is more to come. We're at the top of the staircase. We're all the way in the sky, and he is holding my hand. But now ... But my ... We were standing side by side before. Now he is on the top step, and he is looking at me, and all the angels are behind him. And Jesus is there also.

Michael. Say hi for me, would you?

Karen. And he says, even though I'm leaving right now, I'm always with you.

Michael. And if you want to remember his actual name, it is Yeshua. That was his first name— Yeshua, in Hebrew.

Karen. Thank you. He kisses me on the forehead, and they take him. They lift him up, but he's still looking at me. He said, "Now do your work. Complete your work."

Michael. See I told you. You were the man carrying the jug of water.

Karen. The light's still coming out of my head, by the way. (*Chuckles as she finishes the sentence.*) It is the strangest thing. My whole body looks like light right now. (*Takes deep breaths.*)

Michael. I didn't have to do much here, except tag along. That's cool.

Karen. Yeah.

Michael. You don't need to be sad anymore.

Karen. No. Some of his energy ... He is showing me that we're intertwined. So that was ... I don't understand it in my humanness. But there is something else that is happening on a spiritual level that his energy is going to help transmute universal language to the human brain that I have so that I can share it.

Michael. Ok.

Karen. And that's why I must write it on the computer because I can't conceive it. I must just sit there. I can't say words, but it comes out of me though.

This ended the session connecting with James. I feel at peace that we are able to connect.

Meet Ace.

Chapter 14

Regressing

· ·

We balance karma when we take actions that
offset things we did in past lives.
We release karma when we correct the underlying beliefs,
attitudes or character traits that first caused us to create the karma.
—Robert Schwartz, *Your Soul's Gift*

January 27, 2019

We are at Rumbus Beach in Antigua. My friend Marianne and I won a free spa vacation with my Aveda Pure Privilege points. We are enjoying the ocean breeze and the sound of the waves crashing onto the shore. I am sitting in a gazebo writing. Over to my left is a hammock. To my right, Marianne is sunbathing, reading, and relaxing. There is a cool breeze. The temperature is approximately 85 degrees Fahrenheit. I feel at ease. The Caribbean Sea is a beautiful blue. The air is cool and fresh. I am transcribing the recording of my past-life healing session about the karmic bonds between me and James.

This was recorded on January 18, 2019, with Michael Brady. Before the session, Michael shared this insight: "Time outside of the material realm is occurring at the same time. From James's perspective, he is available to you anytime that Karen's personality thinks of him. He's right here again. Time and space have nothing to do with our connection. When you think of James or anyone else who is no longer on this physical realm, you can connect with them instantly. It is instantaneous when your consciousness pays attention to this or is brought to it by something or some stimulation from the other realm. All time is here now. Once the soul leaves the body, it means that the soul is available to us, even if the soul has moved on to its next incarnation."

To me it seems like a part of James' soul can connect to me here on this plane if I bring him to mind, because who I am is not Karen. Karen is just one part of my soul—one personality that my soul has expressed over its existence. Michael begins by asking me to close my eyes and take deep breaths:

Michael. If you think about deep sighing breaths, you will immediately go into deep full breaths that involve the bottom of your lungs, not just your chest. And you utilize your breath—the tool that God gave you for relaxation. Take a deep breath to shift your body into relaxation out of tension and your mind from conscious focal activity to unconscious diffusional activity—in other words, to go from your conscious to your unconscious mind.

And this happens spontaneously at night when you go to sleep, when you go to bed. You alter your breathing spontaneously from rapid to shallow to down to slow and deep. Your thoughts shift along the way from the normal way you think during the day to that sort of slower pointless drifting quality of thought—until, at some point, you just drift completely away, and you're in what we all call sleep. And then you come up and start your dreams and cycle through your night. Restore yourself and rest your body and recharge your batteries. Do all those other things that we do in our unconscious states of being in mind.

So, you can allow yourself to feel that shift going on. And my voice goes with you wherever you are, and you just try to relax down into your body. Relax down into the place where you sleep—where you dream. And in your dreams, where you see, and you feel, and you do any number of things that you're not able to do in your normal waking state.

And when you feel yourself able to drift down into your heart center, take your right or your left hand and place it there and anchor yourself to your heart center. Once you feel yourself anchored very strongly and firmly with your heart center, you could move your hand back down if you want to or you can leave it there. Either way.

And take a couple of deep breaths and breathe through your heart. Breathe in your heart, and then exhale out through your heart—releasing any stuck, old contaminated, no longer useful energy, feeling, or emotion—so that your heart center, your heart, can open and the energy that is sustaining your existence can flow in and out freely from your heart. Just as the air travels freely in and out of your lungs as you breathe the air molecules in and out. The energy we'll call chi or prana can breathe in and out of your heart and sustain and feed and nourish your heart. When you feel that your heart center is nice and open, nourished, you can nod a couple of times to acknowledge that to yourself.

Karen. (*Sits in silence. Breathes deeply. Nods after a few seconds.*)

Michael. Good. In your heart center, think about, remember, connect with James. Connect in your mind in your third eye with him on a positive pleasant space and time that you had together. Say hello. Feel him being present here and now with you, in your heart. See and perceive and communicate with him through your third eye—through seeing him in your mind's eye, through your mind's eye.

And ask him if he feels it's good for you now to look at the lifetime from which you and he formed the contract you have with each other in this life and see what he says. If he affirms, he thinks it's a positive and useful thing for you to do, just nod your head for me to let me know. And if not, with your eyes closed, you can talk to me and tell me anything that is pertinent about that.

Karen, *waiting in silence for nineteen seconds.* He said yes.

Michael. Good! I want you to take ten deep intentional breaths. And I can speak directly to your unconscious mind as you do that and say that it is most important that your unconscious mind utilize those ten deep breaths to take you back from this life to a different life of your own—a past life, a past time, a different place in time than this place in time. And one in which you were present with and involved with James.

The person you know in this lifetime as James. And that lifetime that you and he as a soul decided to come back in this lifetime from, the connection between this life and that past life. Whenever you find yourself as you do those ten intentional deep breaths, in your mind's eye, in a different place and time than this life, the thing for you to do is to look down there in your mind at your feet and find them. And when you find your feet, when you look down in your mind and find your feet, nod your head for me to let me know. Be aware that there is no reason why, if you want to or need to speak to me, with your eyes closed that you can't do that.

Karen, *nodding her head after a few seconds.*

Michael. The thing I want you to notice about your feet now is, Do they belong to a male or a female?

Karen, *responding immediately.* They belong to a female.

Michael. Very good.

Karen. A little girl.

Michael. A little girl. Okay. Is she barefoot? Or is she wearing shoes, some sort of shoes?

Karen. She's barefoot.

Michael. Good.

Karen. She's got curly blond hair.

Michael. And how is she dressed?

Karen. She's got a little dress on. She's got a white thing around here (*points to the area around the neck*). She's white. Very pale. She's probably about five years old.

Michael. What color is her dress?

Karen. It's like a plaid pink.

Michael. Uh-huh. With a white collar?

Karen. Yeah. And there is a little sash around the ... (*Motions to the midsections.*)

Michael. Around the waist?

Karen. The waist.

Michael. Yeah, okay. What color are her eyes?

Karen. They're blue.

Michael. As you look into this little girl's blue eyes now, what impression does she make on you?

Karen. She's gentle and kind.

Michael. She is gentle and kind. And how does her gentleness and kindness make you feel?

Karen. She's playful now.

Michael. How does she affect you? How do you feel in connection with her?

147

Karen. It seems like she … (*Takes a long pause.*)

Michael. Is there something about … that you're struggling with?

Karen. I'm seeing her, and I'm seeing her body and her feet, but I'm not seeing anything else around her. So, I just saw, ummm. She looked up, and I saw … like … country. I'm trying to figure out where we're at.

Michael. Okay. I want you to take a couple of breaths and let go of all that, except for her. Just see her in front of you. Can you do that?

Karen. Uh-huh.

Michael. Okay. Okay. And let me lead you.

Karen. Okay.

Michael. You're a strong independent type in this life, aren't you?

Karen. Uh-huh.

Michael. Be patient with yourself, and I'll get you there. She's five years old?

Karen. Uh-huh.

Michael. Is she indoors or outdoors?

Karen. She's outdoors.

Michael. She's outdoors. What kind of day is it?

Karen. It's a warm, sunny day.

Michael. Good. What part of the day is she in? The morning? Lunchtime? The afternoon? The evening?

Karen. It's probably around noon.

Michael. Around noon! Very good. Now, see her dress. Take in her from her head to her toes. And now take a deep breath, and you can let your perspective shift. Go from the outside to the inside and become even more connected with her—to her feelings, her attitudes, her thoughts. You can lookout through her eyes—her blue eyes—and see where you're at now. You're outside. Are there any buildings nearby?

Karen, *pausing.* There's like a barn.

Michael. There's a barn nearby. Okay. Is it a barn that she knows? Is it a familiar building to her?

Karen. Yes.

Michael. Yes. Is it her barn? Her family's barn?

Karen. Uh-huh.

Michael. Is she here for a purpose? Near the barn? Has she come to do something here?

Karen. It seems like that's her house next to it.

Michael. Yeah. Okay. Sure. We build the barns next to the houses, don't we?

Karen. Uh-huh.

Michael. So she sleeps and lives in the house. Has she come out to the barn for a reason today?

Karen. She's just out in the yard playing.

Michael. She's just playing. Okay. Very good. Is she happy?

Karen. She's happy.

Michael. Very good. Now you can let your scope of knowing and seeing about her expand. You have a sense of the time behind her standing there in the yard and even the time ahead of her as you need to as we move forward. Do you understand?

Karen. (*Acknowledges nonverbally.*)

Michael. What kind of relationship, as she is five years old does, she have with her mother?

Karen. Her mom just came out on the porch, and she ran up there and basically hugged her. It's a good relationship. It's nurturing.

Michael. Good. And she feels safe with her mom?

Karen. Uh-huh.

Michael. Good. And she's happy most of the time?

Karen. Uh-huh.

Michael. What kind of relationship does she have with her father? When she's five years old?

Karen, *taking a long pause.* Her dad is kind of reserved, sitting at the table in the kitchen, just reading the newspaper.

Michael. Is her dad a farmer?

Karen. Yes.

Michael. He works here on the land that he lives on?

Karen. Uh-huh.

Michael. All right. Is she an only child? Or does she have siblings?

Karen. There's a brother.

Michael. There is a brother. Is he older or younger?

Karen. He seems to be older. Maybe a couple years older, like seven.

Michael. And how did she feel about her older brother?

Karen. They're close. They played together. That's their whole life.

Michael. Good.

Karen. A very simple life.

Michael. Uh-huh. Okay. Now let's look at the most dramatic experiences of her first five years of life. What comes to mind when I say those words to you?

Karen, *pausing for thirty-four seconds,* I'm waiting.

Michael. Uh-huh.

Karen. I'm waiting. Okay. So she gets hit by a car.

Michael. How old does she look or feel to you when she gets hit by a car?

Karen. It seems like it's right around that time.

Michael. Yes. That's true. I don't doubt that. So, you looked ahead rather than behind? Didn't you?

Karen. Yeah.

Michael. Because she really didn't have anything traumatic of importance happen to her in her first five years of life, did she?

Karen. No.

Michael. Okay.

Karen. But it was shortly after when I saw her.

Michael. Yes. Yes.

Karen. When I looked down at her feet, it was within that time period—maybe within that year. She's running outside, and there's a truck—an old-looking, old truck. This is down a country road, and he's speeding, and (*pauses*) she's wearing the same dress! And she gets hit.

Michael. Maybe it's her favorite dress. Maybe she wears it as often as she can.

Karen. Ohh. She doesn't make it.

Michael. Take a deep breath. I want you to slow down and back up.

Karen. (*Takes a few deep breaths, so loudly she can hear herself over the recording.*)

Michael. I want you to back up to the morning she gets up when she gets hit by the truck. Can you do that now?

There is silence for four seconds.

Michael. What's the first thing she does when she gets out of bed and she gets dressed?

Karen, *after a few seconds*. She is in the bathroom with her brother, and they are laughing, and they're brushing their teeth. And they are poking at each other.

Michael. Who started it?

Karen. He started it. (*Giggles out loud.*)

Michael. Does he normally start it?

Karen. It seems so.

Michael. Okay. So, he is a prankster—a trickster?

Karen. Yes.

Michael. He's always doing something?

Karen. And then, the mom is yelling at them to hurry up and get to the breakfast table.

Michael. Uh-huh.

Karen. They sit down. (*Pauses for four seconds.*) They're eating.

Michael. What does she eat that morning?

Karen. They are having eggs and (*takes a deep breath*) grits maybe? Some sort of white grain.

Michael. White grainy something.

Karen. And ummm ... the mom is pouring coffee for the dad. The dad is kind of ... just serious. He really doesn't interact with the kids that much.

Michael. Uh-huh.

Karen. But he loves them. The dad gets up and goes outside after eating. He's in the yard now. He's over by the barn.

Michael. What did the kids do after they eat?

Karen. So ... I'm following this thought. (*Pauses and then continues a few seconds later.*) He's over by the barn, and he's doing stuff. There is hay, and apparently there are horses. (*Pauses in silence.*) Um ... so, he's picking up piles of hay, and he's putting them on the back of this trailer thing. It's wooden, old school. (*Pauses again, and there are a few seconds of silence*). Back in the day.

And the kids run outside now, and they're playing. They're running around the yard. She's got her favorite doll. Her brother is taunting her, and he grabs the doll. He runs across the street. There's nothing out here. There aren't any houses anywhere. She's complaining to her dad that her brother is across the street. He's yelling that he's going to throw the doll in the creek … or running water. Her dad is telling him to get back here. John—John is his name.

Michael. Okay. He's yelling at John to come back.

Karen. And to cut it out!

Michael. Is the road dirt?

Karen. The road is dirt. There isn't any (takes in a sharp gasp of air)

Michael. And their house faces the road?

Karen. Yes.

Michael. And the barn is right there?

Karen. The barn is right next to it, but it's recessed a little.

Michael. A little bit behind the house, yeah? This is a very common way that farms are built, by the way, in the United States for a long time.

Karen. Really? (*Pauses in silence for a few seconds.*) And the dad ignores them because they're just kids playing.

Michael. Uh-huh.

Karen. Then John says that he's seeing frogs over there by the river. She's running toward her brother now, away from her dad. She's running to see what he's seeing … and to get her doll. (*Waits in silence for a few seconds.*) Out of nowhere, a truck comes.

Michael. How does that happen? Does the road by their house have a bend on it or a hill nearby? How does the truck come out of nowhere?

Karen, *waiting as seventeen seconds pass by*. Yes, it's coming down the hill.

Michael. Okay. And the road is tree lined, so it's not necessarily in sight? Too soon? Before the truck arrives in front of the house? Or the farm?

Karen. Yes.

Michael. And the guy is driving fast?

Karen. He's going really fast, and that's why I can't see … I can't see how he got there so quickly.

Michael. Right.

Karen. I don't think she … I can't see because I'm her.

Michael. Right. She doesn't see the truck at all until it hits her? Or she sees it, and it is too late?

Karen. She doesn't see it. She doesn't see it and it hits her. It gets her … Good, old-school truck— like a collectible looking thing.

Michael. Yeah. Umm-hmmm. And does she die immediately? Is she killed instantly?

Karen. Yeah.

Michael. What happens after she leaves her body? Does she leave her body before it hits the ground?

Karen, *taking a deep gasping breath and then breathing deeply for several seconds*. She leaves her body after it is flat on the ground.

Michael. And what does she do when she leaves her body?

Karen. She goes over to her brother, who is coming over to her.

Michael. That's right.

Karen. But she doesn't realize that ...

Michael. She's dead.

Karen. She's dead.

Michael. What happens next?

Karen. He is bending over her body, and he's crying and he's—

Michael. Does she see that? Her body is on the ground, and she's not in it.

Karen. Yeah. And she's like, But I'm ... but I'm right here.

Michael. Right. She still doesn't understand she's dead, does she?

Karen. Uh-huh. The mom comes running outside. The truck is stopped ... You know? Obviously! Her body is pretty much ... uhhhh ... it's an ugly sight, but, uhhh ... the mom comes over. The dad comes over with the mom. The dad picks her up, and he's got her in his arms. He doesn't realize that she is dead. The mom is hysterical. The brother is scared.

Michael. Look at what happens over the next hours to the next three days after she's hit now. Does she hang around? Does she stay close to her body or close to her family for a while?

Karen. Yeah.

Michael. Who does she gravitate to during that time?

Karen. Her brother

Michael. Her brother? What about her brother? Why does she gravitate to her brother so much?

Karen. So she's in ... they are in the hospital, I guess. She's like ... she's going in and out of her brother, and she doesn't understand what is happening.

Michael. She's going in and out of her brother?

Karen. Yeah. She's just moving energy, moving through him.

Michael. Does she try to get inside him? Does she merge with him in some way? *(there is a pause, silence.)* Or is she trying to make contact with him?

Karen. Yes.

Michael. All right. But she can't, can she?

Karen. No.

Michael. He doesn't perceive her, does he? He doesn't feel her?

Karen. No, No. And he's crying ... he's sobbing!

Michael. Is she trying to give him comfort?

Karen. Yes, but he ... he's blaming himself.

Michael. He's blaming himself for her coming out on the road?

Karen. Yeah.

Michael. Because he stole the doll?

Karen. Uh-huh.

Michael. As a prank? Let yourself now look ahead with her spirit, her soul. How long does she hang around? How long does she stay present with her brother—after she leaves her body?

Karen, *waiting in a long silence.* I see him like a young man, maybe in his twenties.

Michael. And she's still with him?

Karen. And she's still around. She's in that house. She's not going anywhere.

Michael. Okay. And what does he do in his early twenties? Does he stay in the house or does he leave?

Karen. He's there. He's now working with his dad on the farm.

Michael. Okay.

Karen. He's very remorseful. He doesn't ... A day doesn't go by where he's not thinking of her—of the way they use to play or the bond they had.

Michael. He misses her?

Karen. Yeah.

Michael. He feels guilty?

Karen. He feels guilty.

Michael. Responsible?

Karen. Yeah.

Michael. Does that prevent his heart from healing over all those years?

Karen. There is an emptiness of his heart that never leaves. (*Cries.*)

Michael. Has he not let anyone else in after his sister dies? Is that why that emptiness is there? Because he won't let anybody else in?

Karen. Yeah. He ends up being a single man on the farm with his ... helping his parents ... and just living. That's his life. He doesn't get any closer to anyone else.

Michael. How long does her brother live his life?

Karen. Maybe into his fifties.

Michael. Can you see how he comes to his passing out of his body?

Karen, *waiting in a long silence.* He's alone in that house

Michael. When he dies, he's alone in that house?

Karen. Yeah.

Michael. Is he conscious and aware of his passing when it occurs? Or does he die in his sleep?

Karen. He has a heart attack.

Michael. Okay. During the day when he is up?

Karen. Yeah, he is sitting on the sofa.

Michael. Is she present when he passes? Is she there in the house with him?

Karen. (*Sobbing, affirm nonverbally that she is there.*)

Michael. Has she been there the whole time?

Karen. (*Nods, affirming without words.*)

Michael. She never left him?

Karen. (*Continues sobbing and affirms again nonverbally*)

Michael. What happens when they were finally able to perceive each other as he leaves his body? He does perceive her at that point, doesn't he?

Karen. (*Cries out loud.*)

Michael. Let your heart feel what it wants to feel.

Karen. It's like undying love. He carried that his whole life, because she looked up to him so much. And he carried that guilt his whole life because he felt (*pauses for a moment of silence*). He punished himself because he felt like he took her life. Then he sees her at the end, and it's undying love. They just came together. Their energies just meshed.

Michael. And what happened when they came together? Was everything okay?

Karen. Peaceful. It was peaceful and loving. It's just *love*. It's just a feeling of deep, deep love. He realized that none of that was real—that he thought she was gone. She was never going to leave him because she loved her brother soooo much. (*Cries.*)

Michael. And her brother is your James, isn't he?

Karen, *sobbing*. Yes.

Michael. Do you see a connection? A relationship between her story with her brother and your story with James?

Karen, *taking a few deep breaths*. How he died so suddenly?

Michael. Right. Just like you died. Just like she died. Very suddenly. That's the same isn't it?

Karen. Yeah.

Michael. What is the favor that her brother is returning to you now as James? Can you see that? (*Allows for a long space of silence.*) What is James helping you understand in this life as Karen that she helped her brother understand in his life when he died?

Karen. It wasn't his fault— none of it. And the reality is that she was never gone.

Michael. Is that the gift that you've received from James in this life?

Karen, *weeping*. Yes.

Michael. It's tit for tat, isn't it? In the same way that we incur debts with each other—tit for tat—we also receive gifts from each other, tit for tat.

Karen. (*Breathes in and out deeply and continues to do so while Michael speaks.*)

Michael. A complete something is accomplished in a relationship between two souls or two people on this plane each time that is realized—a tit for tat.

Karen. Say that again.

Michael. Something is learned and completed about understanding love each time when two souls or two people in a lifetime complete a tit for tat with each other.

Karen. (*Breathes deeply out loud.*)

Michael. If it is a negative tit for tat—you hurt me in a lifetime, and I come back and hurt you in a lifetime—we wear out that way of trying to love each other so badly the next time around until we start learning how to do it better or more positively. Do you see how that works?

Karen. Um-hmm.

Michael. But it is all tit for tat. It's all about relationship—two people, two souls back and forth. Relationship. The conversation exchange. The creation of energy through moving back and forth between each other. This was a favor being paid back. You, she, the little girl, didn't cross over until her brother arrived at the end of his life. She was never able to get his attention—to get through to him. She tried all those earthly years to get through to him, and he couldn't perceive it. He couldn't feel her. He couldn't feel the connection until he came out of his body. But she hung around until he could feel her connection to him, and she could tell him that it was okay. She could be present to him again. He could feel her presence again. And once he did that, he knew that all those things he worried about in his life or blamed himself for in life—

Karen. Were not real.

Michael. Or the things he thought about in his life were wrong. So, he did not have to come forward in his incarnations with that guilt or those messed up thought forms. Do you see?

Karen. Uh-huh.

Michael. She did that favor for him after she died, before she left. She wouldn't move on with her own game. You didn't move on with your own game.

Karen. Huh.

Michael. Until you took care of him. His heart! And James has done the same thing for you in this life, hasn't he?

Karen. Yes.

Michael. Isn't it fascinating how that works?

Karen, *breathing deeply*. So he's moving on.

Michael. Yes. He doesn't have to spend your whole life here.

Karen. Because he understands that I got it. I got the lesson because I stayed around. I understood that on a soul level already.

Michael. You're getting it. That's right.

Karen. I understand that it wasn't real.

Michael. He's been hanging around for a while after he left his body—probably until at least the last time that you and I worked together.

Karen. Yes.

Michael. To let you know, to help you remember what you already knew.

Karen. Yes.

Michael. So he only had to hang around for six months. You hung around for several years.

Karen. Yea, wow.

Michael. And it's another beautiful example of how karma works—tit for tat. It's about relationship and what goes on in relationship. We're learning how to love ourselves and the other along the way.

Karen, *waiting for seconds in which the space is filled with silence*. And both or our souls completed that level of growth. So that's why he said what he said to me when we were going up your staircase.

Michael. Uh-huh.

Karen. And he said—and I can't remember the exact words but I'm going to go back and listen to all of that because I have some serious writing to do—he said, "You have to finish the work you've come here to do."

Michael. Yeah.

Karen. And then like the whole sky lit up with light that was coming out of me from—the lightning strike. (*Voice trails off as she takes in this aha moment.*) So being present in the reality now with the experience is important because (*taking a long pause*) he's gifting me with that—with the gift of actually waking up.

Michael. Yeah. I think that's right.

Karen. In my lifetime.

Michael. Yeah, I think that's right.

Karen. So letting go of everything—false concepts and beliefs

Michael. Yes. You're here to teach people about heart centers, about love, aren't you? And you've got a hell of a powerful message and a way to do that.

Karen. (*Takes deep breaths out loud.*)

Michael. So this thought just occurred to me. Your brother, in that lifetime, lived his whole life alone because he felt like he had let you down or wasn't responsible or was guilty for having allowed you to get hurt, right?

Karen. Uh-huh.

Michael. It's important that you don't hold yourself back with Danny in this lifetime and imitate your brother from that lifetime.

Karen. And my brother brought me a gift.

Michael. That's right! He brought you Danny, so you won't do the same thing to yourself.

Karen. To myself, because I would've ... Ahhhh. (*Lets out a long sigh.*)

Michael. Yes, you would've.

Karen, *agreeing.* I would've.

Michael. You would've wanted to do tit for tat the same way, and he made sure that you didn't do that negative part—tit for tat.

Karen. Holy crap!

Michael. Is that cool or what?

Karen. Holy crap! That is it! (*Breathes in and out deeply.*)

Michael. Your brother didn't want you to be lonely in this lifetime, like he was in that lifetime. You're ... really clean and clear at this point?

Karen. Uh-huh.

Michael. And healed? There's no trauma left from the lightning strike is there? It's just a story.

Karen, *reverberating softly.* It's just a story

Michael. Oh God! I keep being blown away by this work. I swear to God. I never know what's going to come out. That was mind-blowing.

Karen. Wasn't it?

Michael. Yeah it was—again. Well, okay. A concept out of a book called *Oneness* that I've been stewing on for the last month is this: Aside from learning how to love each other as a reason we come here, the main reason that we forget our past lifetimes—that we forget who we are, if you will—is that we could come here and keep having the thrill of discovery.

Karen and Michael, *in unison*). Over and over and over.

Michael. Again. And once you leave this plane—six other planes of reality that we evolve through according to the Hindus—that's not a doable thing. This is the only plane where you get to forget so that you can reexperience discovery over and over and over again—because discovery might be, on a spiritual level, a term equal to *orgasm* on a physical level.

Silence fills the room for moments.

Karen. I just received some material from that.

Michael. Good. That's my job.

Karen. And the way that this ... the way that consciousness becomes aware of itself in this reality is through the transformation that's going to happen from being able to have an awareness while you are reexperiencing the discovery.

Michael. Correct, correct.

Karen. What I just happened ... what I just happened? (*Chuckles.*) That's the brain not working right. (*laughing*) That's the stroke. What I just experienced was a shift in my karmic cycle because I was able to have the awareness. Oh God. I like what is happening right now. I was able to have the awareness before I went down the same path of tit for tat in karmic cycles.

Michael. Yes ... yes. Awareness is the only thing that can break karmic cycles.

Karen, *breathing deeply*. Oh my God. This is so good, and I am glad that I am recording it.

Michael. Me too. Awareness is the only thing that can break a karmic cycle completely, and that qualifier is probably important to be in there "completely." You can partially break a cycle by completing it tit for tat, but you're still going to carry emotional baggage, emotional residue forward— even if you do tit for tat, and you're even functional.

Karen. With awareness, I evolve to the next level in my soul's growth.

Michael. The only way you can completely clear your old energy is with awareness.

Karen. Yes.

Michael. And I'm just learning this stuff too. So I mean, I'm like a paragraph ahead of you or a page and a half maybe sometimes. But don't get the impression that I've had this book in my pocket for a long time. It's not true! I'm in active discovery phase right now in my life—ways that are blowing my mind.

Karen. Yeah. We must just stay on the path.

Michael. Yeah ... and know that we're on the path in the first place, which is the big part. And we've got to know that.

Karen. Oh yeah. We knew that. We knew that from yay big (*Motions with her hands, implying from childhood we knew this.*)

Michael. We both knew that.

Karen, *taking deep breaths.* That was powerful. Do you agree?

Michael. Yes, I do. That was hugely powerful.

Karen. Wow! So now it makes sense why he said to me, "Now you have to finish the mission that you came here to accomplish." Now it is crystal clear in my mind.

Michael. And women are emerging out of the Age of Pisces as we go into the Age of Aquarius. Things go from end to end cycles. Okay?

Karen. Yes.

Michael. We also have been dominated for four thousand years—the age of Aries and then the age of Pisces. Women are emerging as the Age of Aquarius opens. You're the pioneers of the Age of Aquarius. You in a female body is not an accident in this lifetime. You are a voice and an image that people are going to look at and pay attention to because you are female.

Karen, *sighing*. Yes.

Michael. Female power is ascending or reascending appropriately as it should. So you are here to be, in my opinion, a spiritual spokesperson for the emerging female energy.

Karen. The unconscious? Like you read in my chart that first day? The twelfth house stuff.

Michael. Yes, yes. You are here to be an emerging authority.

Karen. Authority?

Michael. Authority is a word that goes with Capricorn. It's a male-like, structural, governmental—you know—this sort of thing. You're creating the foundation of a new tradition in the opening phases in the Age of Aquarius. What you talk about, what you teach, what you bring people to awareness about is going to be forming a foundational structure that probably covers the next two thousand years of our learning—which is the stuff that you and I are talking about, these karmic truths and the spiritual understanding and how things work. You're a Capricorn bricklayer in this lifetime.

Recording ends.

***

I was heading over to Maureen's home to visit her one day in the past months. It was after my hair appointment with her daughter Angie. Thunder started rolling outside as my appointment was being wrapped up. I was nervous, and Angie sensed this and volunteered to pull my car up to the front of the salon. I reluctantly agreed. I didn't want her to be out there. Anxiety crept in as I watched her pull the car up through the glass of the retail section in the salon. She seemed fearless. I was appreciative that she did this. I am aware that others don't experience this intense fear of thunderstorms that I do. According to Alexa, the odds of being struck by lightning are one in 13,500.

"How does lightning form?

According to Planet Science, "A build up of positive charge builds up on the ground beneath the cloud, attracted to the negative charge in the bottom of the cloud. The ground's positive charge concentrates around anything that sticks up—trees, lightning conductors, even people! The positive charge from the ground connects with the negative charge from the clouds and a spark of lightning strikes" (www.Planet-Science.com).

I headed over to Maureen's home after the hair appointment. I know that I'd never feared lightning in my entire life—until I did! If you've lived in a state where summers are filled with daily thunderstorms, it's not unlikely to take the danger of this natural phenomenon less seriously. My PTSD symptoms remind me of the reality of the nature of lightning. It's not just this beautiful spark of light that lights up the sky; it's a force of nature that must be respected. As I pulled up into Maureen's driveway, the thunder was rolling above. I felt my body shaking in a way that I have not been able to control. I sit with it; I am uneasy in my own skin, and there is no changing what is happening in my body.

I sat in the car for a while, watching the rain pour down. I shared this with Dr. Toms as he shared with me that his dogs curl up on him shaking helplessly. Their instinct and connection to nature is most accurate because the force of nature is superior.

Fearless as she is, Maureen dashed out the garage door and got me out of the car and into her garage. She closed the garage door. As I entered her home, she picked up a piece of paper and handed it to me. Maureen mentioned that this had been found on Mark's (her deceased husband who took his life unexpectedly and tragically) iPad when he'd passed. She mentioned that I needed this, and so too did Danny. As I sat down and settled into reading the page she'd handed me, I realized that the message was also coming from James:

> Death is nothing at all. It does not count. I have only slipped away into the next room. Nothing has happened. Everything remains exactly as it was. I am I, and you are you, and the old life that we lived so fondly together is untouched, unchanged. Whatever we were to each other, that we are still. Call me by, the old familiar name. Speak of me in the easy way which you always used. Put no difference into your tone. Wear no forced air of solemnity or sorrow. Laugh as we always laughed at the little jokes that we enjoyed together. Play, smile, think of me, pray for me. Let my name be ever the household word that it always was. Let it be spoken without an effort, without the ghost of a shadow upon it. Life means all that it ever meant. It is the same as it ever was. There is absolute and unbroken continuity. What is this death but a negligible accident? Why should I be out of mind because I am out of sight? I am but waiting for you, for an interval, somewhere very near, just around the corner.
>
> Unknown, All is well

Chapter 15

Understanding

· ·

I reflect on this information in the months to come. I recall the day James pulled up in my driveway. I was standing in the kitchen looking out through the windows as he got out of his car and walked in front of the car toward the passenger side. Danny got out of the front passenger side of the car. I realized Petey was out. I turned and walked into the living room and put Petey in his cage. James knocked on the door. As I opened the door, he mentioned that he was here to install the bathroom sink and asked where the bathroom was. I motioned in the direction of the bathroom and mentioned that it was around the corner to the left. He moved past me in the direction of the bathroom. He was a couple of steps past me when Danny entered the room, and I made eye contact with him. His right hand reached forward, and I immediately moved my arm up, reaching forward in response. We shook hands, and he introduced himself. I responded, "I am Karen," and immediately turned to James and said, "Then you must be James?"

James shook my hand and immediately continued toward the bathroom to install my bathroom faucet.

Danny and I chatted while James was installing the sink. Danny was easy to connect with. It felt like I knew him. I shared about all the home projects that were done on the home recently. As I expressed the concerns I had about the wall that was botched up in the bathroom and the fact that I had to pay someone other than the original contractor to complete the work, Danny empathized with me and expressed that these are not uncommon things when getting construction work done on a home.

We talked, and then Danny shared that he was helping James in hopes of becoming more skilled at plumbing. He also shared that he and James were best friends, roommates, and coworkers.

I spent time with Petey when I wasn't chatting with Danny.

Once the sink was installed, James demonstrated that the sink didn't overflow and that the overflow mechanism was working by filling up the sink. Then he stooped down to look under the sink and to show me that, while the water was running, there were no leaks under the sink. He did this by wiping the area around the pipes with a cloth and had me touch the dry cloth to verify that it was not wet.

As he showed me the cloth was dry, our eyes met. That was the first moment I made eye contact with James. In that moment, something occurred energetically between us that I cannot explain. I felt confused, and after agreeing that everything was installed correctly, I walked out of the room perplexed, moving quickly past Danny as I returned to the kitchen. Danny noticed my reaction as I walked out of the room and later mentioned to me that he'd shared that with James.

Before they left, I inquired about replacing the small hot water heater under the kitchen sink with a large tank that could be housed in the laundry room. I mentioned that the bath was never hot enough, and I ended up boiling water to add to my bath. James looked at the hot water heater and advised that he could increase the temperature and that I didn't need to install a new hot water heater. I was okay with that and he made the adjustments. That night, for the first time in nine years, I was able to take a steaming hot bath. I soaked, and my muscles were in heaven.

Later, I texted James and thanked him for making the adjustments to the water temperature. He mentioned that he could do any plumbing work I would need to have done in the future. I was grateful that I'd found a plumber, and James and Danny were honest, genuine guys.

In the weeks that followed, James and I connected via text. I was at the beach with my friends Shawn, Matt, and family celebrating

Matt's birthday. I mentioned this to James, and he shared that he loved the beach and that he was "a fish." We agreed to have a beach adventure sometime.

On June 24, 2018, James wanted to go snorkeling and asked me if I would like to join him on a trip down to Siesta Key. I said yes.

After the accident, when Marie dropped me off, I immediately got out of the drenched clothes, and then we sat on the couch for a few minutes. We both knew there weren't words. Marie was worried about me refusing to be checked out at the hospital. She was worried about me being in shock. She asked me to not worry if I didn't hear from James's family and expressed that it may not make sense that I'd survived. I felt it to be a heavy burden and didn't want to believe that James was actually dead. This could not be reality.

Marie gave me Danny's phone number and urged me to contact him and share the details of what had happened and assured me that doing this would make me feel better. I was devastated, in shock, overwhelmed with disbelief, and physically exhausted. My last meal was over twenty-four hours prior.

As soon as Marie left the space and silence in the room enveloped me and I couldn't catch my breath, I texted Danny. He mentioned he was at Sarasota Memorial Hospital. I expressed that I was so sorry that this horrible freak accident had happened. I wanted to share what had happened with Danny and asked if he would like to have a phone call the next day or would prefer to stop by. He decided to stop by after work on Monday.

Danny entered the home, and we hugged each other. I expressed how sorry I was. We sat down on the sofa, and Petey immediately flew onto Danny and never left him. I shared, and we both cried. I showed him the palm tree that had fallen over in the back yard that morning, and we were both befuddled by this. It was eerie. It seemed so odd—I was standing there looking out the window; the wind was not blowing, and nor was it raining at the time. I also shared the pictures of the rainbows that we'd seen on the drive home.

Danny shared how empty their home felt and how Ace had been meowing constantly and waiting; it was so sad. Danny mentioned that there was going to be a memorial, and he would send me the details.

In the weeks to come, I invited Danny over to have dinner with me most nights. The house was filled with space, and I felt relieved every time he came over. The heaviness inside me had swallowed up all of the spaces in this home, and I couldn't escape the overwhelming fear that had overcome me. It was only when Danny shared details and stories about James that I felt a sense of relief. I was desperate to fill in the blanks and learn anything about the beautiful human being who had touched my life for a brief moment.

Danny and I grieved, cried, and shared. He was there for me, and I was there for him. He continued to stay by my side, and we found friendship through all the discoveries about my health and how the lightning strike had impacted my brain. He saw me at my lowest. He helped me to see that there was value in living because I really didn't want to live. I was angry. I was confused. He was so comforting and kind. We grieved together.

I wanted to make sure that Ace would be okay. I offered to take him. Ace came over and spent a couple weekends when I felt an overwhelming need to take care of him and make sure he was not alone. I worried about the bird and the cat being in the same home. My heart said give it time, and they will understand—they are going to realize that we are all friends.

While at the workshop with Rebecca Campbell at the Omega Institute, I meditated and had a clear message that Ace needed to be with me at my home. I came home and asked Danny to bring Ace over for a few days. Ace has never been back to his old home. Ace has been very grateful and loving toward me. I joked about him being my cat therapist through all those months when my brain hurt so much, and I was so depressed. He stayed with me in bed and loved me. We slept for twelve to sixteen hours a day. I am grateful that I got all the sleep back then, since it helped heal my brain.

Ace sees Petey with eyes of curiosity. It seems like he wants to play with Petey. We have redirected him in a positive way, and both pets are now able to exist together in the home openly and know that we are all family.

Danny moved in at the beginning of October. I was on medical leave, and we both needed financial support. Our friendship has grown to deep love, and he is so wonderful to me. Danny has a son who is now twelve, and we are getting to know each other. He is kind and adores me. I am so grateful that I had the courage to let go and trust that life would guide me to that which is for my highest good.

This past year has been the darkest period of my life. I have searched within and without to understand why I've experienced this horrific event. I've often felt like the universe played a terrible joke on me. I wondered if I "thought" I understood the nature of impermanence, and life gave me a test to see if I really "got it."

I am accepting that sometimes there are no answers to questions and the deeper understanding to supplement our experiences. I am understanding that there are acts of nature, and if caught in the midst of a storm, the possibility of being swept up by the storm will be greater. I have the deepest respect for the forces of nature and the power of storms. I am not afraid of anything anymore. There is now a sense of peace about being in each moment comfortably because I truly understand the nature of what it means to say that life changes in a flash of a moment. I am living deeply, loving with my whole heart, being kind and compassionate, and allowing life to guide me to the next moment.

Most importantly, I am holding the people I love and who love me close to my heart. I am spending quality time with them. I am listening and having genuine concern for the things that matter to them. I am kinder to strangers. I am generous and give of my time and my presence.

I enjoy doing random things that may be meaningless to others, like watering the plant in my office every time I work in the office. I am spending more moments being in the present moment with the sound of my heartbeat always in my peripheral. I am grateful to contribute a little good to life every day. I am no longer participating in drama and choose not to gossip or be involved in pettiness. These things don't matter when we are gone. I want to be a positive influence or at least bring positive energy everywhere I go—*every day.*

Chapter 16

Embracing

I attended the Hay House Writer's Workshop in Portland and learned a lot. I am grateful for this experience.

March 25, 2019

I'm heading home. My flight was delayed, and my only option was to take an overnight flight with two stops—Portland to LA and then LA to Miami. I'm on the plane heading to LAX. Ever since the accident on the beach, I've been fascinated with the nature of clouds. From up here, I'm looking down at the clouds and observe the sunlight shining through patches of clouds. I'm curious as to why the sunlight isn't evenly dispersed across the entire cloud bed.

Thanks to physics, I'm certain there is a scientific explanation for this. I also notice how bumpy our ride becomes when we travel through the clouds. Once we level out, at the higher altitude, it almost appears like the plane is cruising across the white cloud bed, highlighting the majestic clear blue sky above.

Clouds

I try to capture the contrast of the sky against the clouds in a few photos, but these pictures do not express what I am seeing as we travel through the sky.

The baby across the aisle is smacking the bag of pretzels against the mom's body. This simple task keeps him preoccupied. Earlier he was restless and crying, and now he's completely content with the task at hand. Looking at this beautiful baby absorbed in the act of smacking the bag of pretzels up and down, fully present and alert, makes me wonder, At what point do we lose our connection to the present moment and become consumed with our past or our future?

The noise from the smacking of the pretzel bag has stopped. Almost immediately, I see and hear a restless crying baby across the way.

The sky outside has blended with the clouds. There is a tinge of blue that peeks through, but there is mostly white spread out over the horizon. I come back to my breath and continue looking out the window. I sense the movement of the plane, and yet my eyes deceive me, as what appears outside seems constant and still. Tiredness seeps in. I begin nodding off and make a conscious decision to be still and connect with my inner being.

Later, I open my eyes to the city lights below. The view looks different once again.

City view

March 30, 2019

I attended the Chari-Tea hosted by Fulfill Your Destiny founder Karen Mertes. I was awarded one of the Business Builder Grants given out to several recipients. Karen, a friend of Marie's for many years, sustained traumatic brain injury as a result of an accident. Lately, I was struggling with symptoms such as head pressure and extreme exhaustion, and Marie urged me to meet with Karen, since she had had similar symptoms and might be able to help.

Karen's advice to me has been invaluable. She helped me to understand the importance of accepting the person I am now. I can love and let go of the person I was before and be with who I am and accept myself exactly as I am. On the days when my head pressure is unbearable, I'm not able to function; it is often Karen's advice that helps me to get through the day. She reminded me that it is most important to rest while my brain is healing, even if I just close my eyes and rest. She also urged me to drink lots of water in order to keep my brain hydrated. I'm very grateful for her friendship and the ability to share with someone who truly understands what goes on in my body and how functioning with cognitive deficits translate in daily life.

Chapter 17

Noticing

· ·

If we know how to preserve and care for our own mind and heart, then thanks to that, our brothers and sisters will also know how to live in mindfulness

—Thich Nhat Hanh, *The Miracle of Mindfulness*

May 6, 2019

I was heading to Punta Cana in the Dominican Republic with Marie. I decide to close my eyes and meditate sitting upright in my seat on the plane. I wrote about my meditation later while on the flight:

> I start my meditation by relaxing my face. I feel my lips stretch to create a half smile. Closing my eyes, I feel my scalp and eyebrows release. I begin focusing on my *in* breath and my *out* breath. I feel the movement of my midsection as I focus on my heart. I feel my heart beating. I am grateful to my heart for never stopping. After a few minutes of watching my breath in my mind's eye, I incorporate the mantra below:
>
> Breathing in—I am breathing in life force
> Breathing out—I am breathing out life force
> I feel peaceful. My mind sinks into the blank screen behind my eyelids. The chattering sounds around me ground me in my reality. I am en route via plane—destination Punta Cana. The chatter

blurs as I focus on the darkness in front of me. The space seeps into my cells, and I become it.

May 20, 2019

It's been my goal to get off the meds. How can I do this in a safe way? I looked at Dr. Ahmed and expressed that I would like to get off the meds because, sooner or later, I will have to accept the reality of who I am without trying to fix myself. And my goal is to be there by the first anniversary.

Initially, he leaned back in his chair across from me and his facial expression made me think my goal was a bit lofty. However, I persisted. As I mentioned getting to know the person underneath these meds, he shook his head in approval. So, we are working together to get me off my meds in a safe manner.

I am starting another med that will help to stabilize the serotonin levels in my body and diminish the symptoms I've experienced from the withdrawals of Zoloft. Our goal is to safely get me to a stable place with other meds—the ones that have helped me with my PTSD symptoms, anxiety, and panic attacks. I am patient and continue to trust Dr. Ahmed's expertise.

As the one-year anniversary of our accident approaches, I am curious to see who I am underneath all of the meds that I desperately needed to help me to function. I want to experience the reality of who I am, and I'm willing to be okay with whatever that reality looks like. After all, this has been my journey, an awakening to life as it is in front of me. Acceptance has been key to this process.

Dr. Ahmed and I came up with a plan. After decreasing the dosage of Zoloft, I began to experience some strange symptoms. I shared the list of symptoms I experienced with Dr. Ahmed. As I did so, I saw the concern on his face. If I could translate his expression, I would say he's thinking I'm nuts to try to get off these meds so quickly—especially with hurricane season approaching. I'd been recording the symptoms I experienced as I decreased the dosage of

Zoloft. These included buzzing sensations in my brain similar to the electrical impulse I'd felt on the day I was struck by lightning. I also experienced temporal pains associated with the smell of blood and many more symptoms, including tightness in my chest.

We agreed that I needed to taper off the meds more slowly and add something that will help with the side effects. In the meantime, my anxiety crept up, and it seemed like insignificant things triggered sadness, and I burst out crying. Getting off the meds has clearly shown me how much good has resulted from taking them. The incident not replaying over and over in my mind has been the biggest benefit of being on these meds.

When I saw Dr. Ahmed initially, he mentioned that the symptoms I had were consistent with the PTSD and that he would be treating me as he would someone who had suffered traumatic brain injury. I breathed in and out and remained still, as I willingly accepted any protocol that would help diminish the dread I felt inside me and allow me to be in my own skin comfortably.

As I get off the meds, Marie reminds me that there has been so much good from taking these meds. I've been able to function, and I am not talking about my own death a lot. I didn't consciously realize I was doing that. It certainly felt unbearable to be alive.

As I detox from the meds, I am becoming more acquainted with the person I am now and acknowledging and accepting myself. I am noticing who I am. I am noticing what works for me. It is hard to see myself struggle to get words out or to find the rest of the sentence that was just in my mind, which has suddenly vanished. Even worse is the inability to grasp a word that is at the tip of my tongue—one I know is definitely in the dictionary in my brain, yet somehow, I cannot locate. This is most frustrating. I keep trying though and this is helping me to find the words. I sometimes find them much later in the day and blurt them out.

There is also this strange thing where I can't seem to remember names. It's sort of ridiculous when I've known a person for years, and the name just escapes me. Or if I am thinking of a person and I can see their face and only the last name comes to mind. Last week, I walked by someone at work and addressed him by the wrong name. I was walking by Orlando's desk and said, "Hi, Carlos," and didn't realize it until maybe an hour later. It's embarrassing because he knows that I know his name, and so do I.

I like to think I am a pretty intelligent person. However, I bring myself back to the goal I had when I set out on this journey, and it was mainly to be with the reality in front of me and to think less. With that said, I would imagine not being able to recall names is not such a big deal.

My friend Maureen said something to me as I expressed my frustrations. "You have to be forgiving of yourself, Karen." I am learning to let go of the person I was and see and accept the person in the mirror as she is. I am kind and gentle with myself through this and have learned to have a sense of humor about myself. I am letting go of any need to hold on to what I used to be. I am noticing my thoughts naturally. I am also acknowledging, *This is a thought.*

I am sensitive to my reaction or thought stream as stories come up from others. I am noticing fear. I began affirming to myself in the past days that, *All fear is an illusion.* As I breathe in and breathe out, I continue to bring consciousness to the thought processes I am having. I am acknowledging that these are my thoughts. My breath is my life force, and it is easier to bring my attention to my breath and focus on my heartbeat, especially after I've been submerged in a whirlwind of thoughts. Coming back to the present moment and the reality in front of me is becoming my new normal. I am at ease with my reality.

According to many philosophers, there is only one method of inner
Creativity—meditation (which is learning
to pay attention, to be detached,
and to be a witness to the ongoing melodrama of thought patterns).
To break away from the ego-level of existence, you may need
To identify with some precision what is going on in your everyday
life, to recognize, perhaps painfully, how your habit-attachments
run you. All of these techniques require basic
practice in being attentive and
in being detached. Meditation teaches us that.

—Amit Goswami, PhD, *The Self-Aware Universe*

Chapter 18

Living in Strength

· ·

*One of the wonderful
things about being alive
Is that it's never too late.*

—Phyllis A. Whitney

Sunrise

February 17, 2019

I decide to wake up early and go fishing with Danny, since this is the best time of day for him to fish today based on the reports of high and low tides. I am not a morning person, and I like to sleep in on the weekends.

185

I see my first sunrise, and it is breathtaking. I've seen many sunsets. This is different. The sun peaks out from behind the horizon. I feel the serenity of the moment. I take in the beauty of the sun coming up mixed with the smell of the salty ocean water now crashing up against the rocks. I am full. This moment is perfect. I hear birds chirping all around. There are pelicans floating off in a distance. I look over, and Danny is smiling, fishing, and happy to be with me. I am so grateful this is my experience.

Pelicans

June 17, 2019

Practicing

Being in awareness requires constant practice. The reward is in the journey. By committing to believing only the reality in front of me over a year ago, I committed to practicing awareness. It continues to be a daily practice. I remind myself daily that there is no result.

The result is that I have enjoyed every moment participated in life. As a result, life in front of me changes. As my awareness expands, so too does the reality in front of me. I'm touched deeply by the marvel of existence. Life is beautiful, enjoyable, and rewarding. It is also difficult and challenging at times. I've chosen to be with it completely—breathing in and out and being aware. I observe and remain aware.

June 24, 2019

I was scheduled to appear in court for my name change today at 2:00 pm. I just arrived home. My last name is officially Maharaj. This is my identity. I sit in silence and write. Today, a year ago, we had our accident on the beach. I wondered if it was just a coincidence that my name change was scheduled today.

I struggled to wake up today. I woke up around nine. As I woke, I felt a heaviness in my chest, and the images from this day last year came flooding through. The images of being struck by lightning have been replaying in my mind over and over in these past days.

I woke up yesterday morning, and the first thing out of my mouth to Danny was, "Why did I survive, and he didn't?"

Danny expressed that he was taller and that I had seen the sparks around his waist.

I replied that it didn't make sense because we were standing next to each other.

The truth was, it will never make sense. In life, sometimes things don't make sense.

I breathe in and out of the heaviness inside of me and acknowledge that this really happened.

June 25, 2019

Last night, as we talked about James and honored his life, I inquired about what that day was like for Danny when he first learned that there was an accident. James and Danny had talked about going snorkeling on Saturday, and Danny was not up to the trip. He could have been there with James on the beach. Danny had been contacted by Philippe as we tried to track down family members while at the hospital. He'd returned the call to the case worker at the hospital and inquired about what room James was in. The case worker had informed Danny that James was struck by lightning and he was not alive. Danny could not believe it.

He mentioned that that first night of James not coming home was so silent. It was unbearable; he was alone. I felt how deeply the loss of his friend had hurt him. As we shared our hearts, we agreed that we'd saved each other in so many ways. We cried together.

I thought about James's mom today and how hard this must be for her. I know so many people have lost someone special. May we all keep the memory of James alive—especially his infectious giggle.

I've stayed true to the process of following my heart and opening to the truth in my heart and in my everyday life experience.

I am certain of a few things:

1. Everything I need to know is available in the present moment.
2. I live now and let go of all preconceived notions and expectations about outcomes in my life.
3. It's important that I live with an attitude of gratitude.
4. Being conscious of my breath and body throughout the day is being in my experience of life.
5. The more present I am with what is happening now, accepting all as it is, even if it is uncomfortable, the more consciously I create my future from this present moment.

August 3, 2019

From the *Everyday Mindfulness* book today: "Each morning when I open my eyes I say to myself: I, not events, have the power to make me happy or unhappy today. I can choose which it shall be. Yesterday is dead, tomorrow hasn't arrived yet. I have just one day, and I'm going to be happy in it" (Groucho Marx).

It is a dreary Saturday. The daily afternoon showers have made their way into my entire days during this past week. On Wednesday, the month-end head pressure was in full effect. The right side of my brain felt like it was pushing up against my skull waiting for a crack, a small space to escape. I awoke exhausted, my head throbbing. I thought, *Ohh yeah, it's the thirty-first. My Ajovy injection for the migraine symptoms will not arrive for two more days. I can do this. I get up and get dressed and go to work.*

I slowly make my way out of bed and walk out of the dark room to face the light of day. I'm aware that Petey's cage in the living room is covered, and he is not a morning bird. I make my way to the bathroom, and Ace accompanies me. I am on the toilet a very long time. As a result, I am late getting to work.

It's around 9:00 a.m. when I arrive. My brain hurts, and I am foggy, yet I attempt to focus on my work. I remind myself that I am in a bubble in the building. I have no idea what it is like outside. This is a good thing. I work. I notice myself hitting a brick wall a couple times when my mind just goes blank. I don't know what I was thinking. I was on my headset on the phone with a payer setting up something that is a normal part of my job for one of our locations. The location is an ASC. I express this to the representative on the phone. He is helping me walk through the online process and does not know what an ASC is. In that moment, I could identify the last two letters in the name of the location—ASC, something surgery center—and cannot recall what the A stands for. I ask him to hang on and I run over to my coworker's desk.

"What's does the A in ASC stand for?"

"Ambulatory," she responds

"I couldn't recall," I mutter as I quickly walk away and say to the representative on the phone that it's an "ambulatory surgery center."

It's amazing how the ability to recall detailed information has improved and the things I actually struggle with are names and simple things that I've always known—easy things that I know but somehow can't locate the info in my brain in the moment. I am usually midsentence, and then I am completely blank. My recall is frozen. This situation is exasperated when I'm stressed. I am no longer able to handle stress, and I become stressed when I'm attempting to multitask or comprehend, and my mind is not cooperating.

In the evening, while driving home, I look up and notice dark clouds in front of me leading the way. I barely glimpse at my phone after my cranio-somatic appointment with Dr. Flo Barber.

It's Danny. He says, "Plz drive safely. It's really bad out I'm worried"

At a stop light, I respond, "I'm in it."

By the time I pull up in the driveway, Danny is motioning for me to drive up under the port.

As I grab my purse and get out of the car, I say, "I saw lightning right in front of me as I was driving down the street."

"The power is out," he replies as he hurries me to get into the house.

As the storm rolls through, we sit at the table. The experience on the beach creeps up as I locate words to make sense of the storm I am witnessing outside. We talk. He shares something interesting—it seems like the lightning is most likely to ground or make contact with physical things right before the brunt of the storm comes through. I agree. This makes sense. I reflect on how things were on the beach that day, and this seems accurate. The lightning came before the torrential downpour.

I start to see the images of the lifeguard's truck when I was grabbing everything as the lifeguard urged me to hurry and get in the front of the truck so we could drive off the beach and get James to the ambulance. The rain was pouring down. Yes, this makes sense. I have better perspective about the semantics of storms now. As I watched the rain pouring down outside, I realized that there was no more lightning and thunder at that point. Neither was there any lightning and thunder right before I got into the lifeguard's truck. The torrential downpour was upon us. My dress was drenched.

As Danny and I sit at the table by the kitchen window, we look out at the storm. I remind him that it does not make sense that I am alive. It seems like we were so close to each other. I stood up and stepped over to the kitchen rug. I begin having flashbacks. I demonstrate how close James and I were walking next to each other, asking Danny to stand about one foot to my right and slightly in front of me. My sense of reality shifts, and before I know it, I'm on the kitchen rug crouched down, showing Danny what it was like as we walked through each image. I am yanked into the emotional experience of dread I often feel since that day on the beach.

I saw the lightning flash on the right side of my head. I express that I am reexperiencing all of it. The event on the beach is replaying as if it is right in front of me. Helplessly, I curl up on the floor, crying. My heart is pounding through my chest. I am on the ground and expressing that I can't feel my body, and I want to save him. I am dying and I can't let this happen to him. I must save James.

I am on the floor looking up at Danny, sharing what it was like in those moments. I'm helpless! Unable to move, I'm fighting with everything I have to move. I'm crawling.

"Why is this so traumatic for me?" I question, weeping.

"It's because you watched a man die in front of you."

Tears roll down my face as Danny waits and watches patiently, allowing me to express the volcano that is erupting inside me. He listens attentively and then reaches forward to help me up off the floor. My emotional body has not caught up to the synaptic connections that are firing throughout my nervous system. I bring my awareness back to the fact that this has already occurred, as my nerves aspire to calm in this moment. I affirm that Danny's theory about the lightning striking first before the downpour is exactly how it occurred on that day because it wasn't pouring down heavily until after we were struck.

I am releasing so much pain, releasing the heaviness in my heart. Danny embraces me. We look into each other's eyes. These beautiful eyes in front of me bring me back to this moment. He breathes in deeply—my queue to breathe. I inhale deeply, feeling my shoulder blades expand as I take in life force and then exhale. We breathe, and the silence fills the room. The room is thick with darkness. Silence fills the space. In one corner of the room, a slight reflection from the candle wick quietly shines through, bringing light into the room. Here we are with each other, in this moment—right now. This is our reality. This all happened.

It's going to be like this in the summer months, I tell myself. I am getting through these changes, and I am breathing in and out of each moment. I am living. I remind myself of this fact often during the day. I am at ease when I am just *being* in each moment. I am anxiety ridden if I begin thinking about the future or the past.

And when this happens, I am present with it, and I am graceful in my acceptance of it. It is not my enemy. It is my reminder that I am strong and brave and courageous and kind. And I am human through these eyes and this body, in this moment. I am humbled by the magnificence of life, graciously finding peace within moments.

I am finishing up my book proposal for Hay House. The deadline is August 23, 2019.

Practicing

I have the freedom to be with
life as it is in front of me. I choose to
see beauty in all existence. I observe my thoughts come and
drift away gently, knowing that my
true reality is in front of me.
I am grateful that life has given me the gift of life.
In return, I show up with
awareness in life.
In effect, I am waking up the spirit in me.
In doing so, I am contributing
to the awakening of the entire universe.

—Karen Maharaj

Afterword

January 3, 2020

My dad passed on his 91ˢᵗ birthday on October 4, 2019. Later that month Poppy (a male green cheek conure) joined our family. I have been receiving transcranial magnetic stimulation (TMS) on my brain since November 6, 2019. Initially it seemed like a roller-coaster ride, and my headaches were daily, as well as the strange smell of blood randomly at different times of day. In the last week, I have felt like my eyes have opened to the experience of life in a different way. TMS not only helps with my depression but has also been helping me tremendously with the memory issues I've experienced since the lightning accident. I am hopeful and willing to give myself a chance at life.

I am grateful to Dr. Kenneth Pages and his wonderful staff. I have spent many sessions with Amy and Sydney and a couple with Leo and Desha. I am always excited to see what the saying of the week will be on the whiteboard written by Brianna. Did you know Did you know that "depression" is an anagram for "I pressed on"?

I am grateful that Danny and I continue to grow in love, and life is simple and easy. I am grateful for the daily support I receive from Danny and for the togetherness we share. We are looking forward to a lifetime of loving each other. I am grateful for my wonderful friends and sisters, especially Marie, Maureen, Erica, Merlin, Maajii, and Portia. Thank you for standing by my side through all of life's changes.

I am so grateful to have the support of Dr. Flo Barber-Hancock throughout the process of publishing this book. I am especially grateful for the cranio-somatic therapy she has performed weekly for relief from migraines. I am grateful she is a positive influence and has influenced me to attend Toastmasters meetings. Dr. Barber's inspiration has given me hope and is invaluable.

I am grateful for all of my health care providers for the continued support they provide for me. I am looking forward to 2020, with hopes that my awareness increases a little more every day.

Printed in the United States
By Bookmasters